STRATEGIC JAYWALKING

THE SECRET SAUCE TO LIFE & LEADERSHIP EXCELLENCE

By

Jay M. McDonald

JAYWALKING
COMMUNICATIONS, LLC

Atlanta, GA

PERMISSIONS

Copyright © 2022 by Jay M. McDonald
Printed and Produced in the United States of America

Permissions Dept., Jaywalking Communications, LLC
7910 Stratford Ln.
Atlanta, GA. 30350
Jay@JayMcDonald.com

Publisher: Jaywalking Communications, LLC
Editor: Steve Williford
Cover Design: Fiaz Ahmed
Interior Design: Greg Hastings
Interior Art: Shea Family Artists

Library of Congress Cataloging-in-Publication Data

McDonald, Jay
Strategic Jaywalking: *The Secret Sauce to Life & Leadership Excellence*
Jay M. McDonald
ISBN 978-0-578-31567-6
1 Business. 1 Title.

Printed on approved acid-free paper
10 9 8 7 6 5 4 3 2 1
First Printing

DEDICATION

This book is dedicated to my parents,
**Bernice "Bunny" McDonald Ritter and
Middleton "Mid" McDonald, Jr.**

Though in short supply, good leadership is found in
the darndest places. From huge corporations to
neighborhood delis, the military, flight attendants,
children at play in the schoolyard. In my case, lessons
gleaned from both the words and example of my
parents about human decency, optimism, duty, and
responsibility were baked in long before B-school, and
are more central to my success than *anything* else.

Lessons like what? Read on.

CONTENTS

FOREWORD

"Ted Turner would sometimes tell me that a problem in business was that most people spent too much time trying to figure out the one way to do something right and ignored the fact that there were most often many ways to do it right. They just needed to pick one and do it."

Several years ago I had just started my job in New York as one of the top executives of Burson-Marsteller, then the largest public relations agency in the world. Soon after arriving, I learned of an internal speaker series held for employees. There were about 800 public relations professionals working in the building, and big-name speakers would address them on a regular basis. The last one, as I recall, had been Henry Kissinger. But Burson-Marsteller was the top corporate communications company of that era and represented all the big-name corporate leaders like Jack Welch, Warren Buffet, Roberto Goizueta, Fred Smith, and Wayne Huizenga, among others. The company could get any speaker it wanted.

I was approached and asked to invite my friend and former boss, Ted Turner, who was at the top of his game. CNN had become a global success, thanks in part for its coverage of the Gulf War. Ted was controversial because he was meeting with heads of state like Russia's Mikhail Gorbachev, and Fidel Castro of Cuba. He had launched his Goodwill Games sports competition between the US and USSR as a reaction to the US boycotting the Olympics. He was on the world stage and shaking things up.

There was some anxiousness about him speaking, specifically concerns about his wisdom in meeting with heads of states of countries that were generally at odds with his own government. But Ted was known as a maverick. He did things different, and they most often worked. Despite some concerns about him speaking, he charmed the audience. Someone asked him what made him think he had the right to travel to Cuba and visit with Castro. He simply said that Castro was the only head of state who invited him to meet, and he was willing to meet with anyone who cared enough to want to meet with him.

"Don't get me wrong," he said. "I know who I am. I'm a businessman. I run a broadcasting company, not even one of the largest broadcasting companies. However, my hobby is world peace. I wish everyone had that hobby." His critics were silenced.

Ted Turner is truly a maverick, and as a maverick, he has often ventured outside traditional lines. He would sometimes tell me that a problem in business was that most people spent too much time trying to figure out the one way to do something right and ignored the fact that there were most often *many* ways to do it right. They just needed to pick one and do it. By the way, doing something in a new and fresh way would stand out from the clutter of all those who were doing the same things the same way they had always been done.

At the end of his speech that day, he taught me a simple lesson that captured his whole approach to life.

The meeting was on the top floor of a New York skyscraper in a large open space surrounded by the offices of the top people in the company. By today's standards, it would be considered wasted space. We jokingly referred to it as the "great hall." It was huge, large enough for several bowling alleys. It worked for large gatherings, but wasn't there for that reason. And, it was on the top floor of the building, meaning that hundreds of people were waiting in crowded lines to catch one of the four elevators.

Looking at the crowd and contemplating the long wait, Ted said, "Come with me." We went to the empty stairs, walked down one flight, caught an elevator on its way up, and traveled in the otherwise empty elevator to the lobby. Was that cutting a corner? Not really. Was there anything wrong with it? Absolutely not. What we did was simply "jaywalking" what otherwise would have been a difficult challenge and solving the problem with ease. Too few people think that way.

There is a boldness and effectiveness in being creative in how best to accomplish goals, whether in business or life in general. "Jaywalking" is often being the mercury in a broken thermometer, the ability to navigate bureaucracy and not allow an organizational chart or customs to impede success.

When Martin Luther nailed his 95 theses on the church door in 1517, it changed the world of Christianity forever. It started the Protestant Reformation. Somehow, I doubt that would have happened if another ordained priest had sent a memo to his boss and worked within the corporate procedure to encourage change. Martin Luther did it big, loud and with a lot of imagination. Nailing it to a door cut through the clutter, and instantly the world changed. It was an example of the effectiveness of jaywalking.

Eleanor Roosevelt and Marilyn Monroe are both credited with making the statement, "Well behaved women seldom make history." The truth in that statement doesn't just apply to *women*, it is a reality of success in business.

Taking chances, shaking trees, doing things in ways they haven't been done before are universal truths when it comes to rising and achieving, particularly in large organizations that typically resist change and are as difficult to shift in a new direction as a herd of elephants.

In my early thirties, I left my job as Ted Turner's publicist and promoter to try to become a more "classic marketer" by joining The Coca-Cola Company. After a couple of years, an associate told me I had really shaken things up. He concluded, "You will either be head of the company some day or you'll get fired."

I concluded I had better get out in a hurry. The chances of running the place seemed slim. However, those who stuck around and kept shaking things up were the ones who rose, but part of that journey was doing things different and taking chances…. a risky proposition.

Jaywalking works. However, it is oftentimes risky, and is also walking a thin wire. Aerialist, Karl Wallenda routinely walked a thin wire high above crowds. He did it hundreds of times safely…. until he fell to his death. There is risk.

Some would argue that only the wealthy or privileged, like Ted Turner, have real opportunity, the margin if you will, to jaywalk. I disagree vehemently. It is easy to portray someone in poverty, without access to knowledge or education, as limited in potential. That could not be less true.

My friend Egbert Perry was born in Antigua as one of nine children of a shop owner who never made as much as $1,200 a year. Society would view his family as living in poverty, but their view was simply that they had no material things. But, what they did have was a strong family, led by terrific parents and a vision for each of those nine children.

In an environment where it might seem there was no way the children could possibly go to college, all nine became college graduates! Egbert graduated at the top of his class at the University of Pennsylvania, as well as its Wharton MBA program. He became Chairman of the Board of Directors of Fannie Mae, the country's largest financial institution, and is CEO of Integral Group, a large national real estate developer. His childhood reality drove him to want to solve the challenge of affordable housing for low-income families. He developed what is called the Atlanta Plan of public/private development of low-income housing, which has now been replicated more than 300 times across the US!

There was no logical path for Egbert Perry to get to where he is today from where he started as a child. But, owing to some miraculous jaywalking, his parents and various mentors not only changed his life, but enabled him to improve the lives of others.

Similarly, Billie Jean King could have behaved when she won her first Wimbledon Championship in 1966. The men made the money in tennis at the time, and when she won her first major championship in England, she was stopped at customs upon entering the United States with the trophy and couldn't afford to pay the import tax to get in the country. She was a woman. Women not only didn't make money professionally in sports, but faced daunting challenges in education and the business world, too.

Billie Jean had plenty of reasons to be frustrated. Playing tennis professionally was her passion, but she needed to make enough money not just to live on but also to cover the travel expenses from tournament to tournament. Also, she understood the challenges of overcoming the traditional bans that blocked opportunities for women.

Growing up, she was a much better baseball player than her brother, and would have liked to play baseball professionally. But she couldn't. She was a girl. Her brother, Randy Moffett became a star pitcher for the San Francisco Giants.

I know Billie Jean well and have seen firsthand her passion and drive to create opportunities for girls and women. I served for many years on the board of her Women's Sports Foundation and had the privilege of lobbying Congress in support of Title IX, the law that says women and girls should have equal opportunities in education as well as school sports.

Billie Jean has almost single-handedly changed the world of opportunity for girls and women, and led the way in breaking the glass ceiling in all aspects of life. Recently, the US Open women's tennis tournament drew higher ratings than men's tennis, and now women stars have equal status of respect as well as finances with their male counterparts.

Billie Jean King did what she had to do to change the world and make life more equitable for little girls. Today, more women graduate from college than men, more women graduate as doctors than men, and more women pass the bar exam to become lawyers than men. She jaywalked her way to success, and didn't accept the status quo.

Jay McDonald hit a nerve when he decided to write his book. It is a lesson in what it takes to truly lead a life of leadership and success. We won't achieve greatness by doing things that have always been done and just doing them the same way but better. Finding new and innovative approaches and figuring out how to jaywalk the traditions that hinder progress is the answer. Read the book, absorb the lessons, and start jaywalking if you aren't already doing it.

There is a risk in jaywalking, but the rewards are worth it when it works. There is immortality in making bold changes.

Bob Hope
CEO, Co-Founder, & Owner
Hope-Beckham, Inc.

PART 1:
First Things First

Chapter 1:
INTRODUCTION

Welcome, I'm glad you're here!

This book may be a gift from a friend, relative, business associate, or perhaps you're taking a leadership or other business course and were sentenced to buy and read it. In the latter case, I apologize in advance… it should have been shorter, funnier, cheaper. That said, your professors will likely find the summaries at the end of each chapter useful, so you may want to pay particular attention to them. Just sayin'. ☺

You may not know me, or anything about me. Let's clear that up quickly so you can get on with the book, forewarned about my biases and shortcomings (I've got both.) My hope is that you will learn a bit more about me in the next few pages, but more importantly, about yourself, life, and leadership excellence. So, what's the book about, who is Jay McDonald, and what does he know about leadership and life? What the heck is Strategic Jaywalking, and why should I care?

Last question first. In life and leadership, jaywalking is thinking differently, creatively, innovatively, getting out of the rut, your comfort zone, being constructively disruptive. It's how you might cross the street if there were no crosswalk or flashing sign to control the process.

Jaywalking is intended to unleash a distinctive competence, with intentionality and strategic purpose. It's consciously (and safely) crossing the streets of life without over-reliance on crosswalks, and contrary at times to the blinking red hand "Do Not Walk" sign. Why? Because we can!

Shawn Corbett, a friend and client defines "Strategic Jaywalking" as, "understanding the path you are 'supposed' to walk but deciding to take measured risk and a different path. Some think it's rule-breaking; others call it living!" With tongue-in-cheek, I've often said I'm a natural jaywalker… and have jaywalked most of my life. I tend to color outside the lines, to think differently, to be an optimistic, yet, true to my banking roots, prudent risk taker.

Leadership journeys are seldom straight-line pathways. Planned or not, we're presented with lots of twists, turns, and opportunities. One size doesn't fit all. Every leadership journey is different. So is every leader. Despite uncommon paths, there are common threads to achieving the most success in leadership and in life. My intent here is to share nuggets of insight and stories showing a variety of ways to accomplish that aim. In pursuit of that mission, I will highlight both failed efforts and successes, mine, and others. We paid the tuition; you get the benefit.

There's no one perfect template for leadership excellence, so it's important to be prepared when opportunities arise. Thomas Jefferson, one of my heroes, once said, "Luck is when preparation meets opportunity." My hope is for you to be prepared for opportunities when they present, whether you're in a major leadership role, aspiring to one, or just want to make significant contributions and enjoy a happy, rewarding life.

Like it or not, and ready or not, we're all occasionally thrust into the role of leaders or role models. It's not a title. Rather, a role tasked with inspiring followers to embrace shared values, vision, and goals. It is best earned, not anointed.

Every day we micro-message our attitudes, actions, and behaviors to those whom we may influence. Our leadership platform may be in the schoolyard, in class, a workplace, a home, or in the community. It may result from a civic emergency or a well-planned career. In the following pages, I'll share my perspectives on both successful leadership behaviors, and actions that may inhibit or enhance your success and happiness.

It is intended for young and old, female, male, and all ethnicities alike. None of us is too special to be our best, or just better. My aim is to give it to you straight from the shoulder without spin, hidden intent, or a lot of lipstick. I'll tell you what I think, what I believe I know, and reserve the right to be wrong. You be the judge.

Allow me to introduce myself. Understanding a bit about me, my life's journey, and the lessons I share will hopefully brighten your pathway to leadership and life success. While this book is about leading organizations, organizational leadership can also be a metaphor for life.

Early Years

Born in Germany to American parents, I moved to Tennessee with my pregnant Mother after my dad was killed in the crash of a military plane he was piloting. (Moms have earned and always get a capital "M" in my book.)

Though I have no intention of ever "growing up," my childhood was largely spent in Nashville, Tennessee. We lived in an 800 square foot, two-bedroom, one-bath house with a narrow central hallway which accommodated exactly one person at a time. Until age fourteen, I shared a bedroom with my brother, Chris. Later, our one-car garage was converted to a bedroom with a bath, so I got to move into what seemed like a penthouse suite. Our family was middle class at best. We had our Mother's love, attended church every time the doors opened, and never wanted for a thing.

Attending school and becoming a young man in the public schools of Inglewood (East Nashville) was a wonderful experience, with terrific teachers and friends.

Mom remarried when I was about five, feeling perhaps that my brother and I needed a fatherly influence, and that she could use some help, too. Through no fault of hers, she made a bad choice in her second husband, who proved not to be a responsible, mature, or kind person. My brother and I begged her often to divorce him, but the mores of the times didn't make that an option in her eyes. So, in many respects, we had an anti-role model in him as a man, father, and leader in our own home. Sometimes we learn from both fortune and adversity.

Born a couple of years after me, my brother Chris and I were partners in mischief and childhood in all we did, and remain proudly connected today. We had the privilege of being raised in a community and an era where trust abounded in our part of the world. We safely played outside from daybreak until dark, without a care, coming home only for a bite to eat. We developed friends from all walks of life, played sports and pick-up street games in everything from traditional sports to kick-the-can and red rover. I've since learned that kids must Jaywalk today in order to play red rover in the "modern", risk-averse schoolyard (if there even is a schoolyard). Yikes!

Creativity, learning to get along and to navigate the real world, and a sense of belonging were all part of our early lives. Common sense was learned out of necessity. We did crazy things, too… think helmetless bicycle races, tackle football (pads optional), and perhaps most dangerous of all, eating ketchup sandwiches on white bread… ugh!

Chris and I stood together in protecting Mom from our stepfather, both verbally and physically. Our reliance on each other made us stronger people. I love Chris and his wife Carol and daughter Julie, and am so proud of his success running private wealth management for Goldman Sachs in Nashville. I'm where I am today in no small part due to our relationship and common experiences.

As a child, I was industrious, always looking for a way to earn a bit of spending money. I mowed lawns, had an ice cream route, painted houses, sold Christmas cards, cleaned boats, and held other odd jobs. At age ten, I had my own newspaper route, two of them, which included the Nashville Tennessean (AM), and Nashville Banner (PM), seven days a week. That was about three hours a day slinging papers. My right arm got more throwing practice than most baseball pitchers.

With a knack for organization, detail, and a tad on the geeky side, I mapped out the paper routes on index cards (yes, index cards) for each block of every street by drawing boxes for the houses/addresses receiving each paper and coloring coding them so my helper and I could deliver the correct paper to the right house. In the early morning darkness, things need to be simple but reliable.

With this small business, I began absorbing both business and leadership principles. First, managing people. My across the street neighbor, Johnny, was my helper, until he wasn't. He was the first person I ever hired, and fired. Unfortunately, he couldn't reliably get out of bed at 4:30 AM, which is a problem for a newspaper deliveryman.

Realizing that Johnny wasn't going to be ejected from the neighborhood by this decision, I handled that business with as much aplomb as a ten-year-old could muster. It left me with an important lesson about the fact that sometimes you do have to sever a business relationship, but don't have to be mean and inconsiderate when you do it…and you just might keep a friend.

I paid 3 cents apiece for daily papers and sold them for a nickel (extra on Sunday). To keep cash flow on the right side of the ledger I had to regularly collect from all my customers. Doing collections as a ten-year-old taught me a lot about integrity, human nature, and persistence in the process, especially the persistence. I had a few customers who seemed to think that the paperboy could tote the note on their newspaper bill, a notion I firmly but politely disabused them of.

We also learned to do the little extra things like making sure customers' papers were dry and easy to retrieve in bad weather, being polite to everyone, and knowing which dogs to avoid. If we had extra papers at the end of the day, I'd look inside the paper to see whose picture happened to be in that edition and try to sell them the extra copies. As photocopiers weren't yet common, this effort usually met with success (more Jaywalking.)

Sports were an early passion for me. I played most sports from an early age, first on neighborhood sandlots then on Little League teams, and in school. Of the many great lessons from sports, the ones that stand out to me involve the connection and dependence on teammates, learning that practice makes perfect (or at least better), and appreciating the pride of being on a team. The privilege of wearing the uniform connotes responsibility. Secondarily, it also fed my math skills as I scoured the sports pages of the newspaper to keep up with every statistic available, while keeping running records of my own performance. It's amazing how much your math skills improve when you apply them daily, without the benefit of a calculator.

Georgia Tech

The need for a good education was heavily reinforced to me from my earliest memory. After high school, I gained admission to Georgia Tech in Atlanta, and enrolled as an Aerospace Engineering student. During orientation, all freshmen were assembled in the basketball arena and told, "Look to your left, now to your right. Only one of you will graduate. Welcome to Georgia Tech. Now, go tour your major."

Armed with this little nugget of optimism, I marched over to the AE School, touring with my new classmates. We observed students in the wind tunnels, saw many hunched over drawing boards making detailed images of wings, jet engines, fuselages, propellers, et al, and watched others in class studying complex formulas which looked too much like hieroglyphics to me.

Peeling off from the group, I asked some of the AE students if this was what they did all day. They responded, "Of course, isn't it great?" Not quite. I did well in math and science in high school, but what they were doing held no interest to me. Perhaps I was more enthralled by the Space Program, NASA, and the fact my dad had been a pilot. In any event, I left the tour, headed straight to the Industrial Management School, and changed majors. Self-awareness told my inner self I was likely to be more adept at business and people than engineering. I've not looked back once.

Despite having made good grades through high school, I nearly flunked out of Tech my first quarter. I've since learned that seems to be freshman de rigueur. High school had come easily for me; thus, I didn't really know how to study. In a program where every day is iterative and you're surrounded by smart people, if you get behind, you're dead.

My first quarter GPA was 0.875 with emphasis on the zero. Pursuing a more 'adult' social life, failing to stay on top of my studies, and a degree of homesickness contributed to not doing well. Luckily, at GT you got three strikes before you were out...Warning, Probation, and Gone. Mom asked me what I learned during the first quarter, and I lamely replied, "How to dress." Bad answer!

This setback got my head straight, and I went on to finish in the top 10% of the class. Counterintuitive as it may seem, another big part of getting my grades up was marrying my high school sweetheart during the second half of my freshman year. It forced me to grow up in a hurry! We moved to married student housing, had our son, Sean, and we both worked. I took 18 hours per quarter while working 30 hours/week at different jobs, the last being in the mailroom at the C&S Bank. I used to say, "If you read someone's mail every day for 3 years, you learn a lot about them."

Ditch Digger

My life was already taking another "Jaywalking" pathway. Initially, our young family had no car. I worked the first summer for Georgia Power Company in the Underground Department digging ditches, laying cable beneath streets, and installing utilities in new developments. There were two students on the crew, a fellow named Richard, and me.

One day as were replacing cable under Peachtree Street at the corner of 5th Street in Atlanta, a lady pulled up to the traffic light in a "Woodie" station wagon full of kids. We were covered in mud, grease, and sweat. I told Richard, "That lady's telling her kids, if you don't study and get your education, you're going to end up like those two guys on the corner." Life is good.

The Mailroom

While employed at C&S Bank my sophomore year, I drove a Ford Econoline van from our downtown Mitchell Street office all over metro Atlanta picking up cash letters (deposits and checks) and mail at our remote locations. One day in mid-March after staying up almost all night for several nights cramming for final exams, I was driving I-285 between I-75 and Roswell Road (the only stretch of 285 completed at the time) to pick up at our Sandy Springs bank.

I fell asleep at the wheel just after crossing the Chattahoochee River and slammed at highway speed into the back of a tractor trailer truck carrying concrete and steel beams. The van collapsed like an accordion, I broke the windshield with my face, and was thrown out onto the expressway in what would have made a good commercial for seatbelts. Luckily, help came quickly.

To my good fortune I was transported to Georgia Baptist Hospital, where the best plastic surgeon in Atlanta happened to be on duty, received 400 stiches in my face, had paint from the truck scraped off my skull, had a broken wrist, two sprained ankles, and a banged-up knee. I was lucky to be alive. When released from the hospital, I could have gotten the starring role in "The Mummy."

This experience gave me a new and different outlook on life. Something about a near death experience causes you to rethink your values and priorities. While serious before, I became super focused and grateful to God for sparing my life. It's a game changer on your priorities, albeit one I don't recommend.

Briefly, my leadership journey prior to my current activities is one of Jaywalking on a pathway I could never have imagined. Hard work was an ingredient of every stop along the way. As mentioned, by getting married in college and having a child, it entailed both working at least 30 hours a week and going to school full-time, taking 18 credit hours per quarter. While working for Georgia Power Company, I also sold men's and boy's clothing for Muse's Clothing Store, and ultimately worked in the mailroom for The C&S National Bank for 3+ years.

Formative Banking Years

Following graduation from Georgia Tech, I took a "gap year" job in the Management Associate Program of the C&S Bank. My plan was to take a "work vacation" and learn as much as possible about banking, finance, and how businesses worked, before attending graduate business school at the University of Virginia's Darden School. The bank carved out a special training program for me, despite knowing I would be leaving for grad school in 15 months.

This "special training" led to my being assigned to Pat Flinn and Herb Dickson who mentored me about financial statements and the language of business in a way few people learn. Once again, someone trusted in me and gave me lots of responsibility at an early age, making me a "straw boss" over people several years older and more experienced than me. We wrote credit memos and analyzed financial statements for loan reviews for the bank's credit committees.

Writing and critiquing these memos and attending senior officer credit meetings was a laboratory for learning for a young person. I was a sponge, knowing I had an opportunity of a lifetime. My apologies in arrears to my first official team, who had to put up with me learning how to lead.

Darden Business School

My young family and I moved to Charlottesville, Virginia for me to attend the Darden School at the University of Virginia and receive an M.B.A. It was a wonderful experience and an opportunity (through a rigorous case method of study) to learn from a multitude of real-life cases about leadership and business challenges.

My resume, (https://www.linkedin.com/in/jaymmcdonald/) says that, since school, I've checked just about every box on the leadership job title chart, and done it in a variety of venues, many of them quite successfully. These vantage points have positioned me to work with and observe many outstanding leaders, and some whom leadership skills completely eluded. Each taught important lessons, some of which were more enjoyable than others. I've often said, I flunked retirement five times… all intentionally. Just like some of you, I can't keep a job! ☺

Following significant leadership, board, and ownership roles in both commercial and investment banking, wholesale distribution, sporting goods, printing, publishing, advertising, sign manufacturing, real estate, SAAS, and wealth management, I was, quite by happenstance, enticed to enter the executive coaching profession.

Executive Coaching

Out of the blue, a friend called and asked if I would coach him. I told him that I had owned and led businesses for over 35 years, and during that time had coached hundreds of leaders, but had no specific training as a coach. I'd likely be committing malpractice. He said, "I just want someone with experience to talk with, bounce things off of, and tell me the truth."

I agreed and sought out two friends in the executive coaching world to help me learn how to be a great coach. After working with me for a while, one asked if I had considered Vistage. He indicated it had a great program, trained, and developed its leadership coaches, and was a wonderful model for its clients. I told him that I hadn't a clue what Vistage is but would investigate it. I learned that Vistage was the renamed TEC Group, which one of my partners at Network Communications was in. I knew his Chair and all his fellow members.

Vistage

For the last decade, I've been an Executive Leadership Coach with Vistage Worldwide, the largest CEO and leadership organization in the world. As an organization, it has over 25,000 members globally. I'm also on several corporate and civic boards, serving as Chairman of two privately held businesses. Every week, I work closely with over a hundred top-level executives across a variety of industries and business forms.

Previously, I co-authored the book, *Corporate Banking, A Practical Approach to Lending*, along with John McKinley, published by the American Bankers Association, and used to train thousands of bankers on how to understand financial statements and lend money to businesses. In retrospect, it was Jaywalking in a relatively staid industry. Our book, national and regional workshops, and training methods changed training for the lending and credit professions.

Family Blessings

I'm truly blessed to be grandfather to Mid McDonald, and the parent of Stacy and Sean McDonald. I was married for 39 years to Jani. Although we grew in different directions and divorced, we remained great friends until her death. Her sacrifices and positive influences were critical to any success I achieved, and certainly to the well-being of our family. A strong, loving partner is an asset to all of life's blessings. I'm grateful for her, my children, and my special grand.

Life & Leadership Lessons

Here are a few life and leadership lessons that stand out for me while Jaywalking through life and business. They'll be further fleshed out throughout the book:

Lesson #1: Be Self-Aware, Know Your Values, Your Strengths, Challenges, And Direction

"If you don't know where you are going, you might wind up someplace else."

- Yogi Berra

An early mentor was my eighth-grade teacher, Irene Zurla. She was literally a drill sergeant, a great teacher, and one who put accountability and responsibility on her students. Ms. Zurla gave assignments for everything one month in advance. It was up to us to be disciplined and organized enough to finish everything on time. (Trust me, that regimen is a load for an eighth-grade boy.)

We had to grow up fast or fall by the wayside. Her trust in us brought out our best! It also helped you learn a lot about yourself. Ms. Zurla was the first to acquaint me with the principle that high expectations beget high performance.

Years later, in the second year at grad school, I took a course in Management Behavior. It was an elective, where we read a couple of books a week(!) on various behavioral topics. The final assignment was to write a paper about ourselves.

Following are some of the questions I asked myself, and then posed to a few classmates for further self-discovery, so I could complete the assignment. You may find them useful in your own self-assessment.

What are your values?

My values are traditional ones which include being responsible, caring about others, hard work, integrity, enjoying life, being humble, and authentic.

Where did they originate and are they valid/true?

Most of my values came at an early age from my Mother and impressions of my father, a West Point graduate and lifetime idol for me, from my teachers, and church. As I tested their truth, they've proven to hold up across time.

Who are your role models, known or unknown to you, and why did you choose them?

My role models were my Mom, dad, Vince Lombardi, Mills B. Lane, and Thomas Jefferson. They were chosen because they represented courage, discipline, empathy, vision, and intelligence.

What are your strengths?
- Positivity and growth mindset
- Good interpersonal skills with people from all walks of life
- Quick study with common sense and street smarts
- Good listener and communicator
- Strategic thinker and problem solver

Your weaknesses?
- Impatience
- Intolerance of bureaucracy
- Strong-willed, assertive personality can get me in trouble
- Direct, straight talker
- Tend to be a workaholic. Need to focus on personal fitness and life balance

Your passions?
- Making a difference in the world through better leadership
- Being a good human being
- Having fun while being intellectually challenged

What makes you angry or triggers you?
- People who don't care
- Arrogance: Folks who think they're better than others
- Negative attitudes
- Unreliability

Why?

These things go against my core values.

What's your Why? Why do you do what you do?

My 'why' is to help leaders be the best they can be. In doing so, they will create other leaders who create more leaders, thus exponentially improving leadership and life throughout the world.

If money were no object, what would you do?

I'd have been a high school athletic coach. It would be great working with and developing young people not just athletically, but as the future of our world by positively mentoring them as influencers, contributors, and difference makers. Selfishly, it's rewarding as, at that age, you can literally see them grow from week to week.

How would others answer these questions? What did they say? What did I learn about my self-awareness?

Upon reflection on others' views of me, I came away with the impression that, in the face of having ample opportunity and talent, I'm challenged by the need to focus, choose how best to direct my efforts, and not scatter myself too much.

Some also said I needed to spend more time and effort with loved ones, and in achieving better self-care.

This introspective look into the mirror was eye-opening and invaluable. It provided insight that helped me to create a plan for the next several years of my life. To this day, I revisit it annually to adjust, make changes, and continue my "jaywalking journey."

As a leader, knowing yourself and understanding others is a key to your success. It is just as important as selecting the folks with whom you'll surround yourself. We are always better when accompanied by insightful people who care enough to tell us the truth.

Lesson #2: Create An Education For Life. Be A Lifelong Learner.

"I went to a bookstore and asked the salesperson, 'Where's the self-help section?' She said if she told me, it would defeat the purpose."

- George Carlin

From an early age, I've always been curious and loved learning new things. On my very first day of elementary school, with satchel packed, I bolted out the door and raced up the street toward school, with Mom chasing after me. There was a slight problem. I had the measles and was quarantined for about a week. (It prepared me for Covid-19.)

Doing well in school was always important, so I worked hard (until my freshman year at Georgia Tech) and especially loved to read. Biographies with the orange covered books were my favorite, as I vicariously lived through these larger-than-life heroes of the past. I imagined being with them, as they courageously built this country and our world.

We need to develop our own intellectual property. A few years ago, I served on a private school board for the Galloway School in Atlanta, founded by Elliot Galloway. Before going on its board, I asked him the school's philosophy. His reply, "We give young people self-esteem and help them become voracious readers. With these qualities they will become lifelong learners and achieve personal and professional success." Ding!

Lesson #3: Develop Walking-Around Sense

"I think everyone should go
to college and get a degree
and then spend six months as
a bartender and six months
as a cab driver. Then they
would really be educated."

-Al McGuire

I was raised on the other side of the river from the wealthy side of town. I like to think that by virtue of that assignment, my brother and I accumulated "street smarts" by learning to get along with people from all walks of life, not to judge others, to make do with what we had, and to find solutions creatively and innovatively. In retrospect, we were blessed by this station in life.

Common sense is not always so common these days. There are some who have wonderful academic credentials but little "walking around sense." My acronym for those is HELP...Highly Educated, Low Potential. Even folks with little street smarts can achieve it by listening and learning from those who do the work where the rubber meets the road.

Lesson #4: Two Ears, One Mouth

> *"You can observe a lot by just watching."*
>
> - Yogi Berra

I learned much about listening from the older role models around me. My brain was a sponge for what they had to say and share. Having to be quiet in church also helped my listening skills. My Mother was a great listener, and no matter how crazy or insignificant the topic, she always had time, no, she made time in her busy life to give us her undivided attention.

It's a form of respect. It requires being open-minded to new ideas. A.P. Giannini, founder of Bank of America, was fond of saying, "God made two ears and one mouth, and they should be used in that proportion." In retrospect, God should probably have given us six ears. Ironically, the words listen and silent share the same six letters, suggesting perhaps that we should just shut up, learn to listen, and listen to learn.

Lesson #5: Develop And Use Splendid Communication Skills, Both Written And Oral

> *"Communication - the human connection - is the key to personal and career success."*
>
> - Paul Meyer

Communication didn't come easily for me. As an infant, I had a German nanny and American parents. According to my Mother, I was a bit confused as to which language to use and didn't speak a word until moving back to the United States at 16 months, and then speaking in sentences. I caught up quickly and haven't stopped since.

In church, as a youth, I often got to speak before the entire congregation about youth ministries. This gave me confidence and proved helpful in overcoming stage fright.

My public-school education was also outstanding, as I learned to write and articulate my thoughts. That's a bit of a bold statement to make in the opening chapter of a book, as you will soon be the judge of how well I do.

At Darden, we had wonderful Analysis & Communication classes, where we had to give speeches often and turn in papers every three weeks at 7:00 PM on Saturdays. Darden's case method forced us to stretch our problem-solving skills and learn to verbally defend our recommendations based on facts, logic, and creativity. I found it of immense value.

Lesson #6: Be Passionate About What You Do, And Maintain A Great Attitude

"Nothing can stop the man with the right mental attitude from achieving his goal; nothing on Earth can help the man with the wrong mental attitude."

- Thomas Jefferson

I've had more role models on great attitudes than one should be allowed, starting with my Mom and Grandmothers. Pastor, Charles Swindoll once said, "Life is 10% what happens to you and 90% how you react to it." From an early age, I learned not to worry about anything that didn't worry about me. If you can do something about it, do it. Otherwise, let it go.

Our attitude is a daily (and sometimes moment-by-moment) choice. Each day we get to choose. I've often asked in speeches whether audience members considered themselves a glass half-empty or glass half-full person. Most say half-full, which, to me suggests the possibility of a third option: Consider that you just may not have a large enough glass…you may be overflowing with optimism. Nothing beats positivity in life and leadership.

Nothing! It's contagious. Be a carrier!

Our health, our very existence is affected by our attitude, so follow your passions; have fun in life. Some of the sickest people I've ever met press on well past their expiration date largely on the strength of attitude. They get up every morning, put their helmet on, and go take their turn at bat, smiling through pain or tears. Some of them get more done than "healthy" people who are half their age, or have more ability.

Once driving through Alabama, I saw a sign on a service station wall. It read, "Work like you'll live forever. Play like there's no tomorrow." Wonderful words to live by. Always connect your head with your heart.

What if money didn't matter? My life's been blessed by having my avocations be my vocations. Luckily, I've had the pleasure of loving everything I've ever done professionally. Perhaps it's attitude, perhaps self-awareness. Mostly, I believe it's approaching life with positivity and optimism…and removing yourself from negativity and folks who are not helping you grow and become a better version of you.

One key to having those opportunities, in hindsight, was always trying to do my best at whatever role or responsibility I had at the time. More than once, this positivity has caused my superiors or other influencers to take a chance on me. I can assure you, it wasn't always my brains or good looks.

By believing in me, these folks built my self-esteem, confidence, and my determination to never let them down. Their faith empowered me to do everything I could to make them look good and to validate their decision. It's amazing how much people will do when others believe and trust in them, and equally amazing, how much responsibility you can wrangle by over-delivering on your commitments.

Lesson #7: Be Serious, But Never Take Yourself Too Seriously

"A person without a sense of humor is like a wagon without springs. It's jolted by every pebble on the road."

- Henry Ward Beecher

When I was young, my teeth were as crooked as teeth could be. My eye teeth were looking down my throat. I didn't smile much in those days. After years of braces, my teeth were straight, and I began smiling ear to ear. It's amazing what a smile can do to energize someone, and those around them. Never miss an opportunity to smile.

It's important to be vulnerable, and to laugh at yourself. We all can be goofballs at times. Never take yourself too seriously. Your smile and authenticity will put people at ease, even in tough situations.

Know when to use humor and use it appropriately. No one likes a good joke more than I. And yes, I've told some inappropriate jokes over the years, for which I've felt the need to apologize. In today's world, we have at once, both increased sensitivities and virtually no off-the-record or uncaptured moments.

It is important that each of us have the empathy to never say aloud anything hurtful, off-color, or intentionally offensive to anyone, no matter the audience. Repeat, no matter the audience. That is especially the case for those in leadership roles. By virtue of the power differential, people won't say anything to you about it, but you risk losing the benefit of the doubt with them, and perhaps their respect and followership altogether. Have fun, while being responsible. Just don't go there.

Lesson #8: Be Willing To Take Reasonable Risks. Bet On Yourself.

> *"One who is overcautious will accomplish little."*
>
> – Friedrich Von Shiller

As infants, we learn to pull ourselves up, to crawl, to walk. We do this by continuously getting up when we fall, by being persistent, and resilient. Trial and error. Over and over. Whether it's walking, doing better in school, in life, or in your profession, we grow through our ups and downs, our experiences, and yes, our failures. Be willing to take on hard assignments that other people don't want, or are afraid of.

Franklin Delano Roosevelt, the 32nd US President famously said, "The only thing to fear is fear itself." It's alright to break a little glass. Learn from it, and move on with a lesson learned, rather than never trying, and missing valuable opportunities to grow and prosper.

From an early age, I was encouraged by family, teachers, coaches, friends, and then later by mentors and leaders. I still am! As a leader, parent, or friend, you'll be amazed at the spark and energy you can provide someone by a word of encouragement or saying thanks, offering a genuine and specific "well done," or by publicly acknowledging someone's effort, talent, or contribution. In retrospect, one of my biggest motivators was wanting to continuously improve… "to progress from failure to failure with no loss of enthusiasm," as Winston Churchill once opined.

In most cases, the worst thing that can happen is you try again. You make another decision or try a different approach. Our best life lessons often come from failure, and failure comes from permitting yourself to take a risk; to bet on you!

Lesson #9: Develop An Ability To Laser Focus

"People think focus means saying yes to the things you've got to focus on. But that's not what it means at all. It means saying 'no' to the hundred other good ideas that there are. You have to pick carefully. I'm actually as proud of things we haven't done as the things we have done. Innovation is saying no to 1,000 things."

-Steve Jobs

Because our Mom was employed full time outside the home, focus came early to the McDonald boys. We learned early on the chores and tasks we needed to do, with or without assignment. We washed dishes and clothes (not together), vacuumed, cut grass, ran errands… and always made our beds each morning (thank you Admiral McRaven: *Make Your Bed*). Our lessons were usually done by early evening. The discipline of responsibility helped to create focus that has lasted a lifetime for both of us. That, and a lot of our attendant success is 100% owed to our Mom's teaching and good example.

> *"Time is the coin of your life...
> the only coin you have, and only
> you can determine how it will be spent.
> Be careful, lest you let
> other people spend it for you."*
>
> -Carl Sandberg

While working hard is a given, working smart is even more important. Prioritizing our commitments and attempting to work in order of priority is imperative.

One way I learned early in my career to prioritize my time was to keep a written time diary outlining time spent on every major activity. I color-coded it with different ink colors as to meetings I scheduled, meetings scheduled by others, personal activities, and priority activities. (I should have invented the Franklin Planner.)

After just a couple of weeks, the ink colors showed me vividly whether I was making progress or not on my time management. Actually, it was more a matter of priority management than time management. As I moved up in banking, I found I was called into more and more meetings... most not needing my presence at all (imagine that).

Finally, I went to bank president, Bennett Brown, and asked permission to stop attending all meetings but for the ones involving my people, bank customers, or credit committees I was involved with. I suggested that for other meeting requests, I'd furnish any needed information prior to the meeting. After assenting to my request and as I was headed toward the door, he said with a grin, "I wish I could do that." Take the initiative to invest rather than merely spend your time.

Often, I hear people say they don't have enough time. After establishing that we all have the same 86,400 seconds per day, I suggest that it's not about having enough time, but about using our time on things that are important to us.

Our only way of making enough time is to stop doing something we are now doing. Many have a "To Do" list, and that's fine. Better than that, rather than a To Do list, on your electronic calendar, enter specific dates and times (with an alert) for planned tasks and activities. Then, as importantly, make a "To Don't" list as a guardrail against straying off your path into extraneous tasks. You'll be amazed at how your focus and productivity improve. Always remember, "No" is a complete sentence. Stop unproductive behavior. Start being productive.

Lesson #10: Exude Leadership Values

"Do not follow where the path may lead. Go instead where there is no path and leave a trail."

– Ralph Waldo Emerson

Life and leadership are about knowing and living our values. When we live and breathe our values, decisions have clarity, choices are easier, and our confidence in our direction is reinforced. More importantly, it builds trust.

My life has been inspired by several role models, many of whom I knew, and others I admired from afar. A few of the later group are: Condoleezza Rice, Abe Lincoln, Steve Jobs, Margaret Thatcher, Winston Churchill, and Martin Luther King, Jr. each for different reasons.

Enjoy Your Read

It's my privilege to share with you my life and leadership takeaways and learnings from a life of both success and setback, a few bumps and bruises, and the opportunity to work with lots of wonderful, dedicated, bright people. It is meant to be fun and informative. You can read it straight through like a novel… or skip around, reading the sections and chapters of greatest interest and benefit to you. Either way, I hope you will find it a valuable resource for developing future leaders and enjoyable lives, starting with your own.

Thank you for reading! Jay

Chapter 2:
JAYWALKING

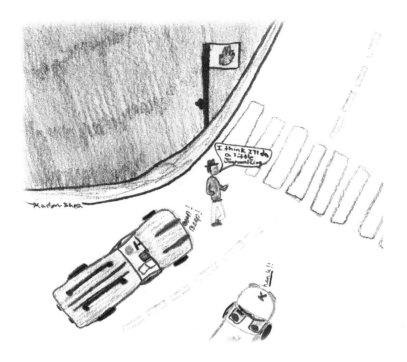

"My wife and I went to a [kindergarten] parent-teacher conference and were informed that our budding refrigerator artist, Christopher, would be receiving a grade of 'Unsatisfactory' in art. We were shocked. How could any child— let alone our child—receive a poor grade in art at such a young age? His teacher informed us that he had refused to color within the lines, which was a state requirement for demonstrating 'grade-level motor skills.'"

— Jordan Ayan, "AHA!"

It's not a big leap at all from children being compelled to color within the lines to adults being required to walk within the lines, and only at prescribed times when crossing a street.

Jaywalking, in the traditional sense, is crossing a street somewhere other than in a marked crosswalk, without the permission of a signal light, if available. If you reside in North America, Jaywalking is likely unlawful in the big city nearest to you. So, if it's unlawful, why do many people habitually do it? For the same reason that kids color outside the lines - there is often a seemingly better, less regimented, albeit less sanctioned, method.

Some of us resent authority and/or having our intelligence insulted... being told what to do, when and how to do it, or not, especially when it's something that we've done since childhood and lived to tell about it (No hot stove effect). Indeed, as a ten-year-old student of Dalewood Elementary School, I attained the rank of Lieutenant (yes) in the school safety patrol, and was assigned responsibility for starting and stopping both automotive and pedestrian traffic every day so my schoolmates could safely cross the street.

Crossing streets only at marked intersections and waiting for a crossing light to advise or permit our crossing is a totally rules-based scenario that takes more patience than some of us are equipped with, or willing to utilize. Presuming humans to being idiots, okay, a few of us are, it ignores the fact that most are quite capable of the sort of analytics required to identify a car a block or so away, assess its speed and path, and calculate the pace required to safely cross the street well ahead of the vehicle. The standard crosswalk's bureaucracy adds cost (time isn't cheap), constricts imagination, and doesn't necessarily de-risk the situation. I've seen more than one inattentive person crossing within the stripes, on the "walk light" nearly get run over, especially when peering at a cellphone. Stuff happens.

What does Jaywalking have to do with leadership, with business, or with life? Leadership is a process of building a team and directing the team's effort, energy, and ability toward a specific objective, e.g., competitive street crossing. In most cases, the speed with which the objective can be accomplished is a prime consideration, a factor bearing financial and other competitive consequences. I'm inclined to wonder why we don't see more individuals and teams exercising their God-given abilities and practicing Jaywalking as part of their work process.

The Fast Eat the Slow

For the longest time, size was the prime determinant of competitive position in business; the big consumed the small. The US Steels, Kodaks, Polaroids, PanAms, Borders's, Blockbusters, and ToysRUs's crushed competitors like garbage trucks backing over so many soda cans. That is no longer the case. Rather, we are in an era where, for as far as the eye can see, many of the big, including several of the aforementioned organizations, and others like them, are vanishing like dinosaurs, as, irrespective of size, the fast eat the slow, by virtue of being the first to discover, to innovate, to truly engage their workforce… to find ways of crossing streets and getting to their destination a step or three ahead of others.

Jaywalking is not a sport. Rather, it's a purpose-driven means, a mindset to proceed apace on a personal or organizational mission, with an eye for using time, energy, and talent smarter, at little to no risk. Repeat, at little to no risk.

Strategic Jaywalking is not playing in traffic for grins and giggles. It recognizes that the "street" before us, our competitive markets can be safely multi-purposed to better accommodate both human and vehicular traffic. It is not unlike what the aviation industry, with FAA cooperation has done by incorporating smarter "traffic collision avoidance systems" (TCAS), thereby safely broadening the use of the skies for more aircraft. It relies on the strength of technology, coupled with a fundamental principle of flight, that pilots and air traffic controllers, shall take all necessary action to avoid collision.

When your destination is immediately across the street from your present position in the middle of a block, if you can safely cross from where you are, why should you walk a full block out of your way to seek the permission of a machine to cross the street, with no return whatsoever on that investment, but for the exercise? Leaders are paid to think… about risk, process, reward, and what's best for the team, the customer, the shareholder, the public at large, and yes, the planet.

Similarly, if you are standing at a regulated crosswalk and there is no traffic whatsoever, why should you be compelled to wait twenty or more seconds for a light to signal your permission to cross? Once again, as adults, why are we deemed incapable of venturing out onto those same streets today, that we mastered in elementary school? *Okay, as adults who are not simultaneously occupied with digital devices!*

In a sense, leaders are like school crossing guards. It's up to us to weigh the risks, cost, benefits, and yes, the laws, and then pull the trigger. It's also up to us to bring about rule and procedure changes as needs and circumstances shift.

"Good leaders don't wait for official blessing to try things out. They're prudent, not reckless. But they also realize a fact of life in most organizations: If you ask enough people for permission, you'll inevitably come up against someone who believes their job is to say "no." So, the moral is, don't ask."

-Gen. Colin Powell

(Made in a video interview with Vistage Worldwide in July 2021, not by some radical theorist, but by former US Secretary of State and one of the finest general officers ever to lead troops in combat for the US military.)

You may be happy to know that serious efforts are underway to decriminalize Jaywalking in many locations. California, which has some of the most stringent regs has taken steps in the state legislature to undo them. Meanwhile…

Upon saving a few extra morsels of time, the question becomes, what *do* you do with it? Too often, as busy leaders with more stuff on our plates than we can say grace over (*I'm from the South, get used to it*) we default to crossing the next task off our list. Though understandable, that is frequently the wrong thing for us to be doing, as there are usually a lot of items on the list that don't belong there.

Instead, we should more often look at those stolen moments as opportunities to invest time and energy into higher yielding activities, like the real, pulsating humans around us… the ones who really get the daily wash out. The ones who look to us as their leader. They are the folks without whom things would come to a screeching halt.

Wouldn't it make sense to do some preventative maintenance, to help one of them grow, to teach them something they've been itching to learn, to show a little compassion or concern, or inquire about a teammate's child who is graduating from high school? You might send a message of appreciation to someone who went out of their way for a customer, or welcome a new team member. You get the picture.

> "What really makes a difference
> in the world is great leaders."
>
> Bill George in "Conversation With Ángel Cabrera"

That's the stuff that makes our jaywalking strategic. It's not the accumulation of stolen moments, but what we *do* with them that matters! It's also the root of competitive advantage, because eventually, it all comes down to whether my team can out-hustle and out-execute yours.

By ensuring that we have a team that is impeccably well-selected, trained, and equipped to execute at pace, we gain that competitive leverage and the delight of our stakeholders, all of them. Mush on!

Chapter 3:
CONTEXT

THEN

NOW

All human beings are entrepreneurs. When we were in the caves,
we were all self-employed ... finding our food, feeding ourselves.
That's where human history began. ... As civilization came, we
suppressed it. We became labor because they named us, 'You are
labor.' We forgot that we are entrepreneurs.

—Muhammad Yunus

And some of us are leaders, the context, demands, and practice of which
has changed more and become more difficult in the last five years than in
the preceding fifty years. The pace of the game is quicker, supply chains
and labor markets are considerably tighter, more complicated, more global.
The expectations of the workforce ("labor" as Yunus puts it), customers,
shareholders, and the general public are different. Yes, higher. Moreover,

the pervasive effect of social and other electronic media creates a much hotter light (or gaslight as the case may be) to be put on management actions. Here's how, why it matters, what we should know and be doing about it.

The Employment Model Has Been Pulverized

Job spans are considerably shorter, more compressed, and overlapping. As noted by Zipcar founder, Robin Chase, "My father had one job in his life, I've had six in mine, my kids will have six at the same time." Obviously, Ms. Chase was speaking presumptively, but her presumption isn't out of reason. Indeed, closer scrutiny of my own LinkedIn page (https://www.linkedin.com/in/jaymmcdonald/) suggests that at present, I, too, have six jobs at one time, because I love what I do, and have flunked retirement five times. Yikes!

There are more "gig" workers and contractors in the workspace (thanks to COVID19, the term "workplace" has become something of a misnomer) than what were once known as "permanent" employees. Very few people go to the same building every day and spend eight hours with their feet screwed to the floor in one spot. Even fewer collect a gold watch upon retirement after a forty-year career with Acme Widget Co. What is "retirement" anyhow?

"My father had one job in his life, I've had six in mine, my kids will have six at the same time."

– Robin Chase, Founder – Zipcar

At the end of 2020 there were about 59 million "freelancers" in the US, representing about one-third of the workforce, a ratio that's widely expected to become the majority by 2027.

As a case in point, roughly half of the 300,000 or so people who work on behalf of Google aren't actually Googlers, as real Google employees are known. Rather, they are temps, vendors, and contract workers, aka "TVC's" who are generally "employed" by staffing firms (e.g., Vaco, Randstad, Aerotek), and whose relationship with Google is at arm's length and an at-will proposition.

Further, there are at present approximately two million people who drive for Uber and Lyft in North America. That's a little less than 1% of the combined North American workforce, and only slightly less than the workforce of Walmart, the largest private employer in North America. Uber and Lyft have not typically considered those individuals to be employees in the classic sense, though the matter continues to be litigated.

What's ironic is that reasonable estimates suggest approximately two-thirds of those people work simultaneously for both companies, representing Lyft on one ride, Uber the next, and perhaps a private limo firm on the one after that. See if you can wrap your head around that. Imagine, for example, that person is you, and you're sitting in a bar, off duty of course, and someone asks, "Who do you work for?" Uh, what day is this, where are we right now, and what time is it?

As British management scholar Charles Handy puts it, corporations need to stop thinking of themselves as employers, and instead, as "organizers of work." I can think of nothing that better represents that notion than the aforementioned Uber - Lyft - Brand X Limo scenario. Organizers of work, a construct that isn't coming in the future… It's been here!

De-Institutionalizing

Thinking back to the point in my career when I was SVP of The Citizens and Southern National Bank in Georgia, had I been found moonlighting in a similar role with Chase, SunTrust, or both, (I wasn't), I can assure you my bank president, Bennett Brown, would not have been as casual and forgiving about the matter. It would have been a short conversation, ending in my having one less employer.

Until about twenty years ago, when sitting at that same bar and asking someone what they did for a living, you'd commonly hear something along the lines of, "I'm a pilot for United Airlines." Today, it's usually more like, "I'm a pilot, ER doc, software developer, hair stylist, plumber, et al," with no tip of the cap to the organization. On so many fronts, we've taken a giant step back from many of the institutions in our lives, employers being just one of them. Churches, governments, and the institution of marriage should take note. To put it in perspective, you don't even need to own or have a long-term relationship with your clothes anymore!

Based on shorter anticipated job spans, and the fact that so many of us have at least an "And One" job, people have different standards and expectations regarding the terms and norms of the deal. It's a bit like getting married for something more akin to the duration of a car lease (a short, 36 month one) than the "till death do you part" variety.

A friend's son volunteered, "We don't marry our jobs anymore. We just date them, and not even exclusively." Thus enter the employment "prenups" that prescribe how things will be unwound when (not if) we terminate this blissful little arrangement, along with diminished loyalty and lack of common purpose. As one might imagine, this development has, among other things, impacted employee engagement levels at their very core. The terms of the deal have changed.

"Being a woman is hard work."

-Maya Angelou

Disproportionate Involvement of Women

Speaking at Fortune's Most Powerful Women Next Gen Conference (June '21), former PepsiCo Chairperson and CEO, Indra Nooyi noted that, despite the facts that "70% of high school valedictorians and more than 50% of college grads are women, only 7% of CEO titles and 2% of venture capital funds go to women." Something's broken. (My comment, not hers.)

Continuing with some serious career advice to women, Nooyi offered the following ideas which, by the way, fellas, work for you, too:

1. Raise your hand for the tough assignments. (There's less competition and higher visibility.)
2. Look at (and understand) the big picture. Don't just be a position player.
3. "Understand the politics in the organization, but don't play the politics of the organization."

Owing to the pandemic-related cratering of school schedules and childcare options, millions of American women have been, at least temporarily sidelined, largely against their will, from the traditional American workforce. Someday, soon I hope, we will better appreciate the fact that schools and childcare are as much an element of infrastructure as roads, airports, broadband, and the power grid.

Trust Enables Speed

Our transition from a long-term relational employment construct to one that is considerably shorter-termed and transactional in nature is a principal cause of reduced levels of trust in the workspace. It's analogous perhaps to a NASCAR driver who would be slowed considerably by a leak in their right front tire.

Workers who lack the psychological safety engendered by trust feel compelled to lift their foot from the accelerator and focus more attention on what's coming up on them from behind, instantly causing the enterprise to lose speed, agility, and competitiveness so essential to performance in today's commercial arena. And we wonder why, despite unprecedented growth in applied technology, rates of productivity growth over the last couple decades have barely budged.

One clear lesson for leaders has to do with the amped up effort associated with recruiting in this environment. Instead of 40+ year careers like the one enjoyed by Ms. Chase's father and much of his generation, workers today spend, on average, something less than four years at an assignment, roughly the equivalent of the time required to attend college and obtain an undergrad degree. As an aside, that's going to bear watching, too, as undergrad enrollments have plummeted of late. Employers have come to realize that, as opposed to the right education, more education (e.g., college degrees) does not necessarily equate to a better job candidate. HR professionals are slowly but surely revising job specs to reflect this reality.

Top college basketball coaches have known for some time what the heightened level of turnover of elite players brings, as they deal constantly with the "one (year) and done" revolving door between their schools and the National Basketball Association (NBA), or WNBA in the case of women players. It compresses everything in the player and team development cycle, starting with the not insignificant level of effort required simply to scout and recruit new talent.

Duke University's men's basketball coach, Mike (Coach K) Krzyzewski, in an interview with David Rubenstein for the book, *How to Lead* offered that, "I work harder at recruiting now than I've ever worked, because you have to do it more often. The top players - you don't know if they're going to be one-and-done, but you know that the really good ones are going to go early. So that means you have to do it over and over."

Think about it. He might spend four years scouting, grooming, and recruiting a single player, beginning perhaps in junior high school, bring them to campus on a scholarship, and in about nine months, they're gone.

Pat Summitt, who coached the University of Tennessee Lady Vols basketball team couched her competitive advantage thusly: "Here's how I'm going to beat you. I'm going to outwork you. That's it. That's all there is to it." In her college coaching career, Summitt-coached teams won 1,098 games and eight national championships! Beat that! More impressive and revealing though is what she said about that record…

"What I see are NOT the numbers. I see their FACES."

Coach Pat Summitt* – University of Tennessee Lady Vols Basketball

*Coach Summitt died in June, 2016 of early onset Alzheimer's. We must continue her fight and rid the world of this disease.

Ironically, having already recruited his own replacement, Coach K is now in the process of advising potential recruits that by virtue of his announced retirement at the end of the 2021-22 season, he, too, is in "one and done" mode after a fabulous career.

Sadly, in so many cases, this "short-termism" has an outsized impact on the entire relationship. For example, not long ago, I was taken aback when I overheard someone say the "quiet part" out loud, mentioning that he makes little effort to even learn the names of his new sales reps because, get this, "they aren't going to be here very long." Unlike Pat Summitt, he neither knew their numbers nor their faces. Predictably, on the premise that you get what you expect to get, his employee turnover rate not only didn't improve - it got worse.

Succinctly summarizing the results of Google's years-long look at team performance, Paul Santagata, Head of Industry at Google suggests that, "there's no team without trust." (HBR 8/24/17). You can neither fake it nor force it. Please make a note of that somewhere.

"There's no team without trust."

Paul Santagata, Head of Industry, Google

The levels of speed and risk-taking required by today's workspace are dependent upon the psychological safety net created by those around us, and absent that safety net, even under the very best of circumstances, the whole thing is going to operate a lot lower and slower. To wit, it's management's job to create and maintain the conditions necessary for that safety to exist, even (no, especially) with those folks who are joining you on the ride for but a short while.

'Amateurs' No More

Again, the Jaywalking thing comes to mind. College athletes used to be recruited with the mindset that they would likely ride the bench for a year or two before earning a starting role on the team, by which time they were fully known, understood, developed, and appreciated. Today, in so many cases, as described by Coach K, the whole ride is over in less than a year. That will doubtless be made more interesting by a unanimous US Supreme Court decision announced in June 2021 granting college athletes the right to be paid for their services, beginning with the use of their "name, image, and likeness."

Suddenly, within one month of that decision, prominent high school athletes were strategically changing schools (coaches) for the purpose of having a more certain path to a college that heavily recruits from that high school coach (more Jaywalking).

Trust is extremely hard to build in a short time, and it's fragile. Historically, it has been developed via our experiential history with an individual or organization, and our back of the envelope assessment as to whether their reality matches up with what's been portrayed or expected.

Imagine yourself as a newly hired aerialist for a Cirque du Soleil show. Let's say that in the early days of your employment, you find the show's operating manager and fellow cast members (to include an aerialist who is to be one of your main "catchers" as you sail untethered through the air) making no effort to get to know you or build trust. How eager are you going to be to let go of the bar and sail across the arena, twenty or more feet in the air on the assumption that this guy has both the requisite skills and your best interest at heart?

Cirque aerialist, Danila Bim, in a fascinating videotaped interview, *How This Cirque Du Soleil Performer Hangs By Her Hair*/TODAY ORIGINALS (https://youtu.be/R8R6ESFMero) discussed in compelling fashion the element of trust at work in her job, indeed with and among all the performers, owing to day to day changes in staffing and work requirements.

To accelerate or at least better organize that process, we see professionals and other individuals in very large numbers using Microsoft's LinkedIn network to portray their body of work and their relationships, or at least those they want to make visible. That doesn't make it a relationship, but it starts the conversation.

According to LinkedIn's own site, in the summer of 2021, they had more than 750 million users worldwide. While that provides something of an appetizer to the relationship, we must work hard to adopt ever-better methods to find, sift, and inculcate into our teams those persons with a greater tendency to be happy, productive, and successful as members of our merry band.

Lest there be any doubt, I am very much a proponent of seeking and hiring only those people who by virtue of values, temperament, preference, and habit "fit" the organization. Let's say you are a retail banker and inadvertently hire a person who has a need to poke their nose in everyone's business, often at the exact wrong time, when coworkers are on task with detail-intensive work, or, when customers are present. The net effect of their behavior is to cause co-workers to be inattentive to detail, and thus annoy customers. And no, before you go there, it's not, repeat NOT a matter of hiring only those who look, act, and sound just like you. Rather, it's about finding those whose personal mannerisms are complementary, even additive to their peer group and work process.

I've learned over a long career that the vast majority of my "regrettable hires" consist of people who simply were bad fits for the organization. Their "hard skills" generally were fine. More commonly, it was an inability to play nice in the sandbox that caused the misfit.

Four Generations in One Workforce

Owing to uneven rates of economic prosperity, patterns of migration, and slower average wage growth coupled with leaned-down pensions, and the ability to work from wherever, we now have four very different generations represented in the workspace simultaneously.

This group is populated by an increasingly diverse mix of people in terms of their race, ethnicity, social, sexual, political, and values proclivities, all of which are a lot more out in the open than ever before. Just spend ten minutes on Twitter or Facebook. Although this diversity in a workforce is a good thing, really, it introduces layers of complexity that leaders are generally unaccustomed to and untrained for, at any level. Starting with personal pronouns, we struggle a lot, just to find acceptable words by which to have simple conversations with one another. Most of us have work to do here, myself included.

What Do They Want?

At the same time, management's expectations of our workforce (us of them and vice versa) are changing as markedly as are the terms of the deal. Consider for example, in Gallup's 2021 Workplace Report, (*4 Things Gen Z and Millennials Expect From Their Workplace*) by Ed O'Boyle, March 2021:

Of the four generations represented in the workforce: Gen X (1965-'79), Baby Boomers (1946-'64), Young Millennials/Gen Z (1989-2001), and Older Millennials (1980-'88):

Gen Z and millennials together comprise 46% of the full-time US workforce

As opposed to Gen X and Baby Boomers, the younger cohorts (Young Millennials, Gen Z and Older Millennials) prefer:

1. That employers care most about employee well-being vs. financial stability. Gallup has identified five elements of well-being: *Career, social, financial, community and physical*" that employees expect.
2. The two younger groups prioritized a preference (not just a tolerance, a <u>preference</u>) to be part of a diverse and inclusive workforce.
3. All four groups place high value on the presence of ethical leadership, though I dare say they define "ethical" differently.

Independent of the Gallup work, a June 2021 survey of 10,000 knowledge workers conducted by Slack's "Future Forum" recorded some hard preferences expressed regarding the desired level of freedom as to where and when work takes place:

- 76% of those surveyed want flexibility on where they work
- 93% want flexibility on when they work
- 56% are open to new job opportunities that may provide them more flexibility
- 21% are likely to jump ship to get that flexibility

As this manuscript is being completed in late Summer, 2021, a tug of war is breaking out between employers, or "organizers of work" and workers, with the primary skirmish line being, "Either give me the aforementioned freedoms, pay me, or eat my dust." In fact, it has become mainstream enough to cause the period to be labeled, "*The Great Resignation.*"

Though these demands have yet to survive contact with a protracted economic recession, it's becoming clear that all the WFH-related toothpaste is not going back in the tube.

All the WFH-related toothpaste is not going back in the tube.

As for the element of social responsibility, Fortune's April/May 2021 issue contained the following rather profound statement by Editor-in-Chief, Clifton Leaf "As far as society is concerned...how a company behaves in the world is now as important as what it sells or produces."

Mr. Leaf's opinion was affirmed that same month via a very public protest by some 200 prominent CEO's to voting law changes that were taking place in 40+ states across the US, changes that ten years prior would have gone (fill in the blank) unnoticed.

> *"As far as society is concerned... how a company behaves in the world is now as important as what it sells or produces."*
>
> Clifton Leaf, Editor-in-Chief, Fortune

Barely two months later, in retaliation, the government of a rural county in North Carolina* voted to immediately remove all Coca-Cola vending machines from county property in protest of the Coke CEO's stance on Georgia election "reform" legislation. You couldn't make this stuff up.

Add to that the matter of having, as every workforce of any size does, disparate political proclivities bubbling just beneath the surface all day, every day, coupled with the fact that more Americans than ever are walking around armed to the teeth. Not to put too fine a point on it, but workplace mass shootings have become too much the norm. As leaders, we get to deal with that, too. Sadly, beefed-up security and hazardous duty pay might be among the next things on the agenda.

"It is important to recognize that people almost never behave like machines. When given directions, we insist on putting our unique spin on them. When told to follow orders, we resist in obvious or subtle ways. When told to accept someone else's solution or to institute a program created elsewhere, we deny that it has sufficient value." Margaret Wheatley - Finding Our Way. She might have called it "Jaywalking."

*It is ironic perhaps that Pepsi, Coke's main soft drink competitor was invented in 1893 nearby in New Bern, NC by pharmacist, Caleb Bradham.

Iron Laws of The New Arena

1. Soft power (built on trust) > Hard (position derived) power
2. Competence = (Professional Skills + Humility + Caring)
3. Principled Messaging Must Overcome Noise, "Alt. Facts", Gaslighting

Deficiency of Skills Required for Success in the New Environment

When CEOs are asked what keeps them awake at night, the strength/length of their bench (especially the management bench) is nearly always a top-two concern. Beginning in the 2020's, this concern has grown by virtue of operating complexities introduced via a host of stimuli (e.g., tightened supply chain), progress across the digital space, and growing societal expectations of employers.

Like it or not, business has become one of the chief repositories of trust in the world, as people regard employers as the entity they look to most often for direction, fairness, and reason, with concern for the environment and social justice on the rise. Concurrently, trust in governments, NGOs and media is decidedly on the wane. In other words, shareholders are no longer the only "public" business leaders must answer to.

Add to that the fact that there just aren't any secrets anymore, to include those about an employer or manager's reputation, and you can see the makings for recruiting difficulty, to say nothing of leadership complexity.

For many years, I've been something of a student of Edelman's annual "Trust Barometer" report, and heartily recommend it as an insightful glimpse at public attitudes toward the major institutions in our lives.

People Have Long Memories

In the spring of 2021, US employers found themselves competing for a shrunken supply of talent from among the ten million or so service workers who had been laid off. It seems, for example, many of the restaurant servers, hostesses, housekeepers, and line cooks had, by necessity, initiated career changes during the layoff. Still others were content to get by on the then available enhanced unemployment compensation benefits. Many (women chief among them) were less able to return to work due to the concurrent implosion of the nation's school schedules and childcare services.

Those leaders who had made more strident efforts to keep people employed, or at least kept contact with and showed a measure of concern for their teammates during the rough patch fared considerably better. Take note: People have long memories of how we've dealt with them during periods of real need.

"This is becoming a massive war for talent. If you are coming out of this and haven't started thinking about whether your employees are going to be remote or not, your competitors are, and they will pick off your talent."

—Jenny Johnson, CEO, Franklin Templeton

Indeed, during the same period, across Europe, governments and businesses banded together and adopted a variety of schemes whereby substantially more employees were kept on status with at least partial pay. The result was that, across the EU, whose aggregate population exceeds that of the US by roughly 100 million, they lost but 2.6 million jobs versus 9.6 million in the US.

Productivity Growth and Worker Engagement Are In Flux (They're Related)

Discretionary Effort

Beginning with a series of workplace studies in the mid-1920's, social scientist, Elton Mayo et al discovered that worker morale and in turn, productivity were inextricably linked to leadership behavior. Specifically, workplace leaders who paid attention to and showed respect by listening to and considering the input and feelings of workers often received the benefit of an extra morsel of effort beyond what was required for people to simply keep their jobs. This eventually led to coining of the term, "Discretionary Effort" by another social scientist, Daniel Yankelovich.

It's an extra (and not insignificant) level of effort that remains entirely at the discretion of the individual. We all have it, and we make decisions throughout our lives, even moment by moment, about how much, if any of it we're going to deploy. It represents the difference between what we must do to remain in the game, and what we can do when we really want to crank it up a notch.

In his book, *The Power of Moral Leadership,* author Roy Holley describes its source: "Trust, loyalty, commitment, discretionary effort. These are attributes that reside only in the heart…the spiritual, deeper dimension of humans. It's not that there is a shortage of these qualities within the human heart… but rather that there are too few leaders with the 'gravitational pull' of moral character and integrity to touch and awaken these qualities in others."

For about three decades, Gallup (and others) have attempted to measure, largely by survey, the propensity of workers to part with discretionary effort via an assessment of what has been termed "employee engagement," the degree of satisfaction, adhesion, stickiness if you will, between the individual and the organization.

In Gallup's survey, levels of worker engagement are survey-assessed and then aggregated into three groups: "Engaged" (typically about one-third of the sampled population), "Not Engaged" (approximately one-half), and the remainder who are what Gallup calls "Actively Disengaged." "Engaged" workers are those who feel that the organization and its leadership are creating conditions sufficient to cause them to want to stay, work hard, and prosper.

The "Disengaged" cohort generally consists of those whose response to the survey suggests that they are showing up and doing just enough to get by, "mailing it in" (my terminology).

At the other end of the continuum, those who fall into the "Actively Disengaged" sector are not only disinclined to do those things (disengaged), but they are also prone to deliberately and destructively throw sand into the gears. It doesn't seem harsh to suggest they are tending toward mean-spiritedness, deserving a ticket to someone else's payroll, preferably a competitor's.

Looking back over the twenty-year period from 2000–2020, worker engagement scores of Gallup's surveyed population have slowly but steadily increased from 26% to 36% "Engaged", with the "Actively Disengaged" cohort dropping from 18% to 14% across the same period. For those who might suggest that the improvement of the Engaged group into the mid–30's isn't exactly bragging territory, I would agree with you.

For those who might wonder, "so what?" consider that:

When comparing top vs. bottom-quartile business units on worker engagement, Gallup found measured median percentage difference (advantage) of:

10% in customer loyalty/engagement

23% in profitability

18% in productivity (sales)

14% in productivity (production records evaluations)

18% in turnover for hi-turnover companies

43% in turnover for low-turnover companies

64% in safety incidents (accidents)

28% in shrinkage (theft)

81% in absenteeism

All results favor the more highly engaged units.

*https://www.gallup.com/workplace/321965/employee-engagement-reverts-back-pre-covid-levels.aspx n other words, it doesn't take an MBA to figure out that this stuff matters, a lot.

Contrary to what one might expect, the 2020 survey, coinciding with the first peak of the COVID pandemic, amidst a rotten economy, massive layoffs, and widespread death by virus featured some of the highest engagement scores throughout history.

One important and I think notable distinction is that, while this period of difficult life conditions caused large segments of the workforce to be sent home to do their work, birthing the "Working From Home" (WFH) moniker, it also caused many leaders and their organizations to step up as never before.

"We're living in an environment where we're having meetings in people's bedrooms. Having a high degree of empathy and listening I think has been really, really important through this crisis."

Chip Bergh - CEO, Levi Strauss & Co.

WHAT?

1. A product of the heart + the mind, Discretionary Effort is a force multiplier.
2. We have entered an era where concurrently, the pace and complexity of the game have quickened, while job spans are shrinking, affording appreciably less time to find, inculcate and bring each teammate to peak performance.
3. Trust enables speed but is slowly earned and easily lost.
4. As workers have less connection with the "employer," organizational loyalty is being subsumed into personal loyalty
5. Building bench strength is a key to organizational resilience.

SO WHAT?

1. Operating at a much faster pace with shorter tenured, distributed workforces, the leader's role is morphing from a supervising work distributor to that of a coach, a full-time coach of the whole person.
2. The requisite skills required by the leader's new role include better communication (especially listening), multicultural adaptivity, recruiting, and far more sensitivity to ESG requirements.
3. Younger generational cohorts, Millennials and Gen Z express strong preferences for choice and flexibility insofar as how, when, and where work gets done.
4. "Soft power", based on trust, is taking precedent over "hard" or positional power

NOW WHAT?

1. Make a "high trust factor" a prime requirement for leader roles, ALL of them.
2. Find ways to be a better learning, and thus more adaptive organization.
3. Regardless of pressure to do otherwise, hiring people who by virtue of pace, preference, and temperament "fit" the task and the organization is, and will always be important.
4. Some of us, me included, should continue sharpening our relational skills, notably listening and empathy. This would be a good time. Let's get busy.

Chapter 4:
THE ROLE OF THE LEADER

A leader is someone who creates infectious enthusiasm."

—Ted Turner

A friend made a simple, yet profound statement when he said, "The business of leaders is people." It's about gathering a team, setting a course, inspiring creativity, building confidence, getting the "wash" out. It's about creating the opportunities and conditions for people to be the best they can be, every day.

With all due respect to systems, processes, and technology, people are the common denominators of success in nearly every organization and industry around the globe. *The business of leaders is people.* Here's how.

Inspiring, Engaging, and Presenting Opportunities Encourages Success

Organizations are basically "cathedrals for human development" where people of all flavors and varieties come together to learn, grow, excel, produce, and prosper. From entry level to the CEO, nothing gets done without someone making a choice and directing, enabling, and/or leading others to act.

Leader as Sherpa

As leaders, it is our job to define success, make it a beacon, and guide others to it. We provide guidance, support, and make success possible by giving people the information, tools, encouragement, and resources they need to win. Let's say that word again, together, out loud… Win.

Not unlike a Sherpa (expert mountain guide), we accompany our team to the top of the mountain, or as close to it as they are able to get, setting rope lines to enable safe ascent/descent, monitoring weather, oxygen usage, providing encouragement, emergency support, and playing traffic cop with other groups on the mountain. Not unlike the Sherpa, the leader's role is often more hazardous than that of their teammates. The risk comes with the job.

When you think about it, winning is important, to all of us. I don't know of anyone who gets up in the morning and says to themselves, "I want to go lose today. I want to go halfway and then turn back. I want to hang out with some really mediocre people." No way. Now, at times we all have a little difficulty finding or maintaining the motivation to take the steps necessary to win, but that's where leaders and coaches come in.

> *"We the people will always accomplish so much more than I the person."*
>
> Chef Jose Andres via NBC

Leaders encourage success by helping others build skills, and thus the confidence to face difficult challenges. Leadership on this level is about inspiring excellence and bringing out the passion, the best in everyone. It can be a hard, crooked uphill path, tiring and messy as hell, but it's so worth it.

Be Careful About Your Assumptions Regarding People and Leadership

Margaret Wheatley theorized that our assumptions about the people we lead, and our primary purpose can, and often do get off track, particularly when we're laboring under an 'Old Story' view of what work, workers, and leadership are all about. In such a construct, *"It is the role of the leader to pump energy into a lifeless mask and… provide the organizing energy for a system that is believed to have no internal capacities for self-creation, self-organization, or self-correction." Margaret Wheatley - Finding Our Way*

It should go without saying, but should you find that you've somehow gotten yourself into such an 'Old Story' organization, or working for an 'Old Story' leader, start looking for an exit ramp, quickly. Be assured that if those on your team feel that way, they will likely do the same.

Appreciation and Acknowledgement Build Trust

> *"Character may be manifested in the great moments, but it is made in the small ones."*
>
> —Winston Churchill

It has been said that the deepest human need is to be appreciated. Whether it's at home with loved ones, a close friend, or in the workspace, appreciation and acknowledgment for a job well done build self-assurance and motivation. As leaders, we provide feedback to our teams through formal performance appraisals, or at least some still do (you should, too). But do we always take the time to really appreciate effort, tenacity, and attention to detail, or just a "good old college try," and do it on a more real-time basis?

How Do YOU Do Leadership?

One of my friends works for Berkshire Hathaway Realty. A while back, she was visiting their Atlanta area headquarters on the 5th floor of a high-rise building downtown, adjacent to the Ritz-Carlton. The office is occupied mainly by administrative professionals, with lots of workstations and cubicles. Team members come regularly to meet with their leaders and to get contracts done.

From time to time, she goes to meet with the person she reports to, and so she walks in one morning. She said that in the lobby reception area there is a very nice wingback chair. She had never seen anyone sit in it in all her years with the firm. That morning as she walked in, she noticed an older, white-haired gentleman seated there.

She walked through to visit and do her business with her associates and mentioned the fellow in the chair to one of them, not knowing who he was or why he was there. She learned that it was Warren Buffett, who happened to be in town on business with Coca-Cola, on whose board he sits. For the uninitiated, Buffett's firm, Berkshire Hathaway has their name on the door. Mr. Buffett had stopped by specifically to compliment their team, and express his gratitude, with absolutely no fanfare. He asked for no special treatment and didn't show up acting like a privileged big shot.

There is a lot of "noise" in our world today, of both the decibel variety, and noise that's created by people and messaging competing otherwise for our time and attention. Sometimes a low-key, forthright approach like the one used by Mr. Buffett can speak volumes without the noise and distraction, almost like a gentle breeze of fresh air.

Just to expand that a bit, I've known a lot of highly successful and significant businesspeople, athletes, entertainers, politicians, et al in my life, and, to me, the ones with the most impressive records tend to be more like Warren

Buffett. Unconsumed by their importance and good fortune, they're down to Earth, knowledgeable, well-mannered, nice. One more time, their Mamas raised them right.

Back to Mr. Buffett's visit, I think that's a great example of presence in a good way, taking the time to add a stop in his day simply to give a shout out and say something positive at one of his companies. Nobody had asked him to come, they weren't expecting him, and he didn't have to do it.

Leaders who acknowledge their people build connections on a personal level that translate into trust and commitment. Showing that you are invested in the success of your teammates gives them an important tool they need to excel. In the decade of the 2020s, people will not work long or hard for those who ignore this critical equation:

> "Work is contractual. Effort is personal. We give it up when, where, and for whom we choose."
>
> Bill Catlette

In my interview recently with Dr. Beth Cabrera of Cabrera Insights (http://cabrerainsights.com/) she was quick to identify a trust gap that was illuminated via the 2020-21 pandemic period. Tens of millions of American workers (many of them women) were suddenly and necessarily trusted to do their work from home (or elsewhere). They (make that we) did so without complaining, and with remarkable levels of productivity. We spoke of Mr. Buffett's visit to the Berkshire Hathaway office, and she was quick to point out that "people perform better when they know you care."

But now that the "all clear" signal has been sounded (or has it), and in many cases the fish are all being summoned back to the tank, the "If I don't see you, I don't know you're working" argument is effectively shot full of holes. She went on to point out that, "Women want hard jobs. They want demanding jobs. They just need to do it on their own terms and have more control over doing their work. I'm thrilled because there's going to be a demand for flexibility that we've never seen before." As one who has extensively studied

---

and written about this aspect of our workforce, Dr. Cabrera knows from whence she speaks.

Coaching the Whole Person

Our lives as business leaders are coming to mirror that of Coach K's in another way. The involvement we have with our "players" is no longer confined to coaching basketball or making widgets, and it doesn't end when the bell rings and the school or workday concludes. Ready or not, like it or not, we have become coaches of the whole person, a role that many of us are untrained for and indeed some are unfit for or unwilling to assume. Not unlike our players, we've got work to do.

Based on the belief that performance excellence in sport can only be consistently achieved as the result of high-level personhood and academic rigor when combined with athletic achievement, Dr. Homer Rice, Georgia Tech's former Director of Athletics was, like Coach K., known for pursuing a "Total Person Program" approach to his work with student athletes. His theory is that the athletic aspect is but one leg of the three-legged stool. You coach the whole player. The program is now carried on by Todd Stansbury, Georgia Tech's Director of Athletics, and himself a Georgia Tech alum and former athlete.

To get ourselves fully aligned with the mission of our work and its place/ purpose in the world takes special people and a lot of dedication, the kind that only arises from the whole person-type approach used in Georgia Tech's Athletic Department.

"It is important to recognize that people never behave like machines. When given directions, we insist on putting our unique spin on them. When told to follow orders, we resist in obvious or subtle ways. When told to accept someone else's solution or to institute a program created elsewhere, we deny that it has sufficient value." Margaret Wheatley - Finding Our Way. She might have called it *"Jaywalking."*

Managements are taking note and feeling the pressure to get their oars in the water on matters they have traditionally chosen to stay out of, witness nascence of corporate involvement in the Diversity, Equity, and Inclusion movement. Providing capable business leadership was already a hard enough job. Strapping on added layers of responsibility and constituents only makes it harder, and the task of finding/developing people for these roles more challenging. I'm in that business, every day, and can vouch that the climb is only getting longer and steeper, with less time to accomplish it, and to recover between climbs.

These changes, together with the evolution of the first line leader role from an eyes-on work distributing "supervisor" to a team leader of disparate, distributed, asynchronous talent fundamentally re-orients the skills and attributes required to perform this role. I cannot emphasize the significance of this enough and would venture that better than half of our first line and mid-level leaders are either ill-suited or untrained for the roles they now occupy. That's likely an understatement.

So-called "soft skills" like adaptability, humility, caring, coaching, creativity, teamwork, communications/listening, and influence are accentuated while hands-on production assistance and direction are reduced. As noted in a May 2021 piece in Human Resource Executive, Faethm Vice President, Stephen Farrell opined that "Automation of mundane, repetitive tasks in legal, accounting, administrative and similar professions will mean that core human abilities—such as empathy, imagination, creativity and emotional intelligence, which cannot be replicated by technology—will become more valuable." More, not less valuable. Oh, and another thing, let's be reminded that soft skills done poorly get hard real fast.

With limited visibility into each worker's process, leaders will need to become expert in starting with discrete production outputs and working backward, without a lot of visibility to the tactical steps that enabled or impeded progress.

At the same time, resultant from the pandemic, first and second-level leaders have been much more involved in emotional support roles for their teammates as bolt-on parts of the leadership job. This will only continue, bringing into play another dynamic, notably that managers who come up two quarts low on empathy will need to be moved to a different assignment. This is but one part of the toothpaste that's not going back in the tube. I'm willing to be wrong, but my sense is that empathy is pretty much a "factory installed" option. You either come with it onboard or you don't.

> *"Adaptability is the new efficiency. In the post-pandemic business environment, talent leaders must embrace sustainable adaptability, the capacity to adapt operating practices in a manner that does not deplete or damage resources."*
>
> Kathleen O'Neill

Return on Leadership (ROL)

In a June 4, 2021 piece for Fortune Analytics, Lance Lambert unveiled a new stakeholder capitalism-focused "Return on Leadership" metric, which ranks the 2021 Fortune 100 (largest publicly held) list of companies on the basis of purpose-driven metrics (https://indiggo.ai/rol-100/rol-fundamentals/) meant to incorporate a broader array of non-financial factors associated with leadership performance.

When the best organizations in the "Return on Leadership" ranking are then examined on a purely financial basis, the data suggests that mastering the larger view of leadership effectiveness is one of the best things we can do for the bottom line of our organizations, a notion that I concur with completely.

This is all going to take a while to balance out. As reported by Gartner in an April 15 2021 article, managements will be on the horns of a dilemma in that some organizations will rely on AI to absorb large swaths of the work distribution and tactical feedback roles, while others will resort to retraining or replacing existing staff.

Consider the fact that most of those who are returning to work after having been effectively self-supervising for a year or more, will understandably bridle at anything that smacks of micromanagement upon their return, hence, some thoughtful discussion about the new order is necessary.

"The responsibility that was shown by all colleagues and workers during the pandemic...they earned, in a way, the right to decide where they want to work and how."

—Francesco Starace, CEO, Enel Group

Work Complexity has Mushroomed

While in naked pursuit of speed in every aspect of business process, we are also adding complexity at an equally dizzying pace. Those two factors don't always play nice together.

Put yourself in the shoes of a Starbucks barista on her (or his) very first day of work. It's 5AM, a line is forming, and you realize that you are the only thing standing between that line of people, (in person, in their cars and on their apps) and their very first cup of coffee for the day, and it better be hot, right, and right now!

Just before taking the first order, you recall that there's something like 87,000 different combinations and permutations of drinks represented on that giant menu board, and that there is extra heat on to keep ticket times to an absolute minimum. No pressure. Here it comes:

"I'd like a quad long shot grande in a venti cup, leave room, half caff, double cupped, no sleeve, salted caramel, mocha latte with 2 pumps of vanilla, substitute 2 pumps of white chocolate mocha for mocha, and substitute 2 pumps of hazelnut for toffee nut, half whole milk and half breve with no whipped cream, extra hot, extra foam, extra caramel drizzle, extra salt, add a scoop of vanilla bean powder with light ice, well stirred. And oh, by the way... I have a free reward for this." Gulp.

Worse yet, imagine that you're the shift supervisor or store manager, and that this customer is tying up your drive-thru lane. Or, that the order comes in Spanish, and your only Spanish-speaking baristas are scheduled on a later shift. Moreover, how do you hire for that? How do you train for that? How do you staff for it? I'm not picking on Starbucks. I LOVE Starbucks, but at some point, all the added bells and whistles are a hindrance to the business, customers, and certainly the team in green aprons who, BTW, usually deserve much better tips. Think about it, would you want to deal with a still groggy, un-caffeinated version of you two hundred times before 8AM every day?

Root Out Needless Complexity:

Not long after Mary Barra's appointment to a senior leadership role, GM was apparently in the throes of internal deliberation over the employee dress code policy which, reportedly at ten pages in length, Ms. Barra apparently thought a bit much.

Amidst all the to'ing and fro'ing, she brought the debate to a close, doubtless to the chagrin of those who thrive on paper, by sending a powerful signal via the company's new dress code policy which (ALL of it), reportedly, is now embodied in the words, "Dress Appropriately" as in, we think we hired an adult. Act like one.

By the way, Ms. Barra's path offers exceptional insight into what women can (and do) deliver in a workplace where they are welcomed, and given significant challenge. As the first female CEO and Chairman of a 'big 3' automaker, she joined the company at age 18, and has since held an impressive array of both line and staff assignments, including some tough jobs like Manager of the Detroit Assembly Plant and Global Head of HR, on the path to the corner office.

Emerging leaders, female or male who have the desire to make it into the C-suite would do well to study and emulate the approach taken by women who've gone before them and absolutely crushed it; people like Ms. Barra, recently retired Xerox CEO, Ursula Burns (who's enlightening new book, *Where You Are Is Not Who You Are* is a great read), Lockheed CEO, Marillyn Heuson, Walgreens new CEO, Rosalind Brewer, Kat Cole, President and COO, Athletic Greens, and Oprah to name but a few.

Plant Before You're Hungry

When you find yourself in a position where a key worker has taken their act elsewhere, growth has unexpectedly created a need for additional staff, or you need to "de-select" someone - for whatever reason - it helps if you already have "bench strength." This refers to the practice of locating, building warm relationships with, and sometimes hiring strong candidates before you actually need them. That way you can hire proactively instead of reactively. I can assure you your judgment is much better in those cases than when a key job has been vacant for a month or more, at which point your focus is simply putting butts in seats.

Further, if you lack bench strength in a particular area, you are far more likely to endure sub-par performance from an incumbent simply because you don't want to incur the pain of initiating tough conversations and possibly replacing them.

Conversely, most companies hire based on immediate need. If someone quits or is let go, the reflex action is to write a job description, advertise the position, contact the best applicants, interview, and eventually hire someone to take on a job that has likely already been vacant for a month or more. This is reactive hiring, instead of proactive hiring. If you think I'm mistaken, ask your recruiters what their "Time to Hire" ratio looks like for core jobs, and which direction it's heading. This is something you should always know, and they will respect you for asking.

When you hire reactively you tend to find only those people who are immediately looking for work - people who need a job right then. You might find someone good, but often, you only find those who have a hole in their dance card that kinda sorta matches yours. That's a much smaller, less exclusive list than you'd ideally like to work with.

On the other hand, if you target key roles and are always looking for people with talent and interests that match those roles, and more importantly, people who are good cultural fits (or adds) for the organization, you have the luxury of looking for the best talent, not just what's available in your greatest time of need. You keep a reservoir of and maintain a relationship with prime candidates who are capable of filling the role. This creates bench strength, breathing room, insurance. Call it what you want. Then, when you need to fill a role, you can choose from the best...from those that you've pre-selected rather than hoping that the Tooth Fairy comes, and good people just fall out of the sky exactly when and where you need them.

It's not unlike the process of selling. Successful organizations don't pause their sales efforts until such time as the bank account is running a little low. No! They're selling all the time, but all that selling is for naught if your recruiting measures don't sufficiently keep pace and allow you to get the stuff produced.

Intentional recruiting also takes into account employer efforts to locate and build relationships with a diverse stable of candidates.

The Healthcare Businesswomen's Association organized a study labeled *Empowerment, Diversity, Growth, and Excellence* seeking the critical success factors associated with superior performance in attracting and retaining women in leadership roles within the life sciences industry. Conducted by Booz Allen Hamilton, the study suggested that, from a 39,000-foot view, their assessment of "the six best practice components required to create the environment for more women to reach their full potential in leadership roles are:

1. "Unambiguous senior leadership support for advancing women,
2. Merit-based culture to ensure advancement regardless of gender,
3. Program metrics to track progress and evaluate success,
4. Recruiting techniques that include a diverse team and diversity targets,
5. Leadership development programs customized to individual needs and,
6. Career and work flexibility models to retain top talent."

Though all those factors are important, I will submit that item #5, the customized leader development (likely with a coaching component) is a real difference maker.

A Lesson Worth Learning From Covid-19

While the pandemic period has doubtless been a period of sacrifice, challenge, and disruption, for those who relocated their work to their dining room, kitchen table, or elsewhere, two things happened: 1) They left behind many of the annoying aspects of corporate communal work, including the daily commute to work, itself, and 2) Perhaps more importantly, many of them experienced interactions with their leadership (some for the first time ever!) that were welcome and appreciated.

I'm speaking specifically of so many of those out-of-the-blue calls, texts, and other messages where someone above them in the food chain was asking not about their work, but about *them! Are you (and your family) okay? Do you have what you need? What can I do to be of help to you?* Some likely needed CPR after hearing that for the first time ever!

Concurrently, many, many leaders and organizations bent or broke their own rules and policies to be more fully supportive of their workforce, economically and otherwise. Where those things happened, it didn't go without notice. In response, absent direct "supervision", many (most?) found it within them to be more productive by getting more work done, which was a good thing, at least until burnout took hold for some. That's a significant residual issue looking ahead, especially in healthcare (particularly in the clinical arena).

Going forward, the questions for organizational leaders will be: 1) What additional lessons can we take from this experience? 2) What does Humpty Dumpty v. 2.0 look, sound, and perform like, and 3) Haven't our teammates earned the right to do their work differently, going forward? What does that look like from the 30,000-foot level? What does it look like from the ground?

As we strive for higher levels of engagement and discretionary effort, here are a few tips I've learned along the way that make it easier to get closer to that 100% mark, or at least out of the mid-30's.

All It Takes Is Patience…Just A Little Patience

But first, as a prelude to the next paragraph on patience, I'll borrow a confessional snippet from the "Springsteen on Broadway" album (Growing Up) in which rocker, Bruce Springsteen, as only he can do, says,

"I come from a boardwalk town, where everything is tinged with just a bit of fraud.

So am I.

"I've never held an honest job in my entire life. Never done any hard labor.

I've never worked 9 to 5. I've never worked 5 days a week, until right now. I don't like it. I've never seen the inside of a factory, and yet, it's all I've ever written about.

Standing in front of you is a man who has become wildly and absurdly successful by writing about something of which he has had… absolutely no personal experience.

I made it all up. That's how good I am."

With that as a backdrop, I'm going to take a stab at this thing called patience, about which I, too, still know too little (references available ☺).

Patience…It's Still a Virtue

The tendency to rush through things to get them completed sooner is nothing new, and our need for speed isn't going to go away. For generations, executives and CEOs (including this one) have been struggling with patience. You and I both want answers now, not next week, and we want to see results and a positive return on our investment instantly, today. This afternoon would be considered long-term.

However, with the goal of giving 100 percent of your skill, attention, and commitment, rushing anything is at best counterproductive, and at worst, destructive. Chronically making demands, outrageous demands at times, on people below us in the food chain, because we can, exacts a toll. (I refer you to the above data on discretionary effort.)

Learning to meter our pace and volume takes practice. The good news? Patience is still a virtue that can be developed over time, I hope, as do the people around me.

Some might posit that being patient is counter to the theme, indeed the very title of this book. Au contraire! Patience, like Jaywalking, is predicated on understanding that pursuit of immediacy in and of itself can be counter-productive, even dangerous. Jumping in front of a moving bus because you think it can avoid hitting you isn't productive, smart, or good Jaywalking.

In situations where your patience is likely to be tested, loosen your grip a bit. That's right, *loosen*, not tighten. It's counterintuitive. Getting the tightest possible grip on a golf club, baseball bat, bowling ball, tennis racquet, your job, whatever, practically guarantees that the velocity and distance of the struck ball or other object will be compromised by virtue of less clubhead speed being generated. You simply cannot swing as freely when you're all tensed up.

The same holds true for us at work. I can attest to the fact that taking a well-timed walk outside and/or listening to a few cuts of favorite music when you feel the tension welling up can work wonders. Try it. I think you'll like the result. And yes, so will the folks around you. (Indeed, large segments of this book were written while listening to songs I've played hundreds of times, and am familiar with every word, pause, and note. Unless the battery in the device is dying, I will not notice the music.)

As leaders, we simply must disabuse ourselves of the notion that we're required to be the font of all the ideas and answers. Not so. Thank goodness. Hard as it may be to believe, we do not have the market cornered on brains and good ideas! Rather than demanding that things be a certain way, turn situations around and start by asking more questions, better questions of your teammates:

"You tell me, what's the best solution here? Is this even a problem that we need to fix? Is that the best we can do? What alternatives and risks can you think of? If you were running this place, what would you do? Tell me more. (No one ever gets angry or annoyed when you invite them to tell you more.) What else have you got? What do you need? How long is that going to take? What help do you need from me, if any? Do I have your Commitment (capital 'C' intentional) to get it done?" When would be a good time for me to check back and see how you are doing and if you need anything?"

Look, you shouldn't be the only one who goes home at night with a tired brain. Besides, if you've got the right people on your team, they are practically itching to show you what they're capable of, their best stuff. Let them do it! Many save it up all day and then take it home with them unspent because we never ask! Don't cheat them out of the opportunity to think, own their work, and show off their talent.

Think Qualitatively Not Quantitatively

In a world where quotas and mathematical equations define success, it's sometimes difficult to think qualitatively, especially for a Georgia Tech/ Darden guy, like yours truly. I tend to think about data and numbers in almost everything I do. But the truth is, when you take time to focus on the "how" and "why" behind output, it's easier to maintain that high level you're looking for. As is true with patience, it takes practice to learn how to "re-train" the mind and there will always be exceptions where the numbers must be the primary consideration.

Make it a point to at least consider how we can improve rather than by how much changes will be worth. Remember, thinking qualitatively doesn't mean you always have to own, birth, or impose the answer; it simply means you should be willing to explore the possibilities, and to enlist the help of others who are craving the opportunity to give it. Sometimes we must take a little risk to learn, stretch, and grow, and encourage those around us to do the same.

I saw this one afternoon on a whole different scale during a trip to the grocery. (I'm a bargain shopper who gets leadership lessons wherever I can.) When checking out, old school style, I was in a lane that happened to have both a checker and a bagger. Occasionally, it still happens!

The checker was a veteran Publix employee, fully proficient in her job, whom I recognized. The bagger was a woman in her mid-thirties I'm guessing. She was struggling not physically, but with the mental part of her job, notably the protocols for bagging fish apart from other food, and poisons separately, frozen with frozen, and those kinds of things. Like my friends at Marriott, Publix does a fine job of hiring folks who have some extra developmental challenges. There was a line of about five people behind me.

After swiping my card, my first thought was to pitch in and "help" her with the bagging, but upon starting to reach for the first item to bag, an inner voice told me to hold up and consider the unintended consequences of doing so. If I start bagging things, that will make the folks behind me in line happy for a minute or two, but what does it do for the confidence of this lady (the bagger), her self-esteem, and future job prospects?

Who am I to take her work, her job away from her? I made a silent bet that she and the veteran checker would figure their routine out, and in the end, all would be fine. This was, after all, a line at the grocery, not a hospital ER. Against my efficiency-driven predisposition, I exercised a wee bit of patience and let the folks in line behind me wait, and test theirs perhaps. I had just found an all-too-rare moment of patience. They could, too.

As I was exiting the store, the checkout area manager tapped me on the shoulder and whispered, "Thank you for what you just didn't do." After I commended her powers of observation, she said something to the effect that she had deliberately paired the new bagger with an experienced checker and that the only way for her to gain confidence was to be allowed to do her job, albeit under the tutelage of someone who totally knew the ropes and was a decent coach. And she added, "The reason I saw you is because I'm watching that situation from a distance. If things get too bogged down, I'll personally go open an adjacent register to smooth things out." Ding! I would hire that woman in a first line management role any day! Never stop recruiting.

Be Like A Steam Iron

And that is a textbook example of what managers get paid to do. A frontline manager was personally overseeing the OJT of a new team member to ensure her success and, at the same time, removing obstacles from her path, not unlike what a steam iron does with a wrinkled shirt or blouse.

Good operational leaders regularly spend a good portion of time smoothing out wrinkles in their arena; more specifically, they notice the things that are keeping their teammates from doing their very best work, and in general making them crazy...bad methods or process, worn out equipment, untrained staff, bad guidance from above, dumb policies, you name it. These are the things that kill productivity, destroy morale, and suck the life out of people. Like a steam iron on a wrinkled shirt, good leaders quietly, relentlessly search these wrinkles out and dispatch them with barely the hiss.

Be that steam iron.

This principle is at the root of what has long been known as "Servant Leadership." In that sense, these leaders see it as their job to make it easier for those around them to do their best work. There's nothing soft about the servant leader stuff. It gets results via the earned consent of the team. In that vein, there are a lot worse things you can do than being an activist for your team and customers. Be that steam iron.

Put differently, world-class college basketball coach, Mike Krzyzewski, aka Coach K suggests that "The very first thing is that to get better, you change limits. And when you at first change limits, you're going to look bad and you're going to fail. At West Point, I learned that failure was never a destination. In other words, figure out why, and then change.

"The other thing is that you're not going to get there alone. Be on a team. Surround yourself with good people and learn how to listen. You're not going to learn with you just talking. And when you do talk, converse. Don't make excuses. Figure out the solution. You don't have to figure it out yourself. That's what we've tried to build our program on for the forty-two years now that I've been a coach."

Author's note: To date, Coach K's teams have won five (5) NCAA Men's Basketball National Championships.

WHAT?

1. We have entered an era marked by considerably shorter job spans where we have appreciably less time to find, inculcate and bring each teammate to peak performance.
2. Despite the increased "need for speed," patience is still a virtue, at the end of the day, it often enables speed.
3. There is no team or team effort without trust. Trust enables speed, too.
4. Building bench strength is a key to organizational resilience.
5. Work is contractual, effort is personal.

SO WHAT?

1. Operating at a much faster pace with shorter tenured, distributed workforces, the leader's role is morphing from a supervising work distributor to that of a coach, a full-time coach of the whole person, a Sherpa.
2. The presence of tight labor markets will reward those who find and utilize non-traditional applicant sources, and like a good fisherman, keep their line in the water.

NOW WHAT?

1. Initiate "always on" recruiting for all core positions.
2. When you find yourself in tense situations calling for patience, loosen your grip a bit, a wee bit. Go for a walk or listen to some favorite music.
3. Find ways to be a better learning, and thus more adaptive organization.
4. If you need to sharpen your coaching skills (I bet you do), this would be a good time. Get busy.
5. Make a "high trust factor" a prime requirement for leader roles, ALL of them.
6. Be the "steam iron" that silently, almost effortlessly removes wrinkles from the path of your teammates.

PART 2:
Required "Factory Installed" Qualities For Leadership

Of the essential qualifications for leadership, some are more the product of nature, while others can be bolted on over time, through a process of nurture. Following is a description of that first cadre, the ones which are "factory installed." If you, or others in your organization are being considered for a leadership role and are lacking in or don't especially enjoy these areas, you might be well-advised to explore other venues for your talents.

Chapter 5:
COMPETENCE
(No whiners or whackos)

*"Humility is the simplest of all
heroic qualities to assume,
and yet the least expressed."*

Adm. William McRaven (USN, Retired)

You must first be a competent human equipped with things like common sense, humility, social skill, courage, thick skin, AND THEN a competent professional.

Leadership is a contact sport where some bumping and bruising (metaphorically) is both allowed and expected. Those who get in the weeds over every slight, insult, or loss have no business in a professional leadership role, at any level.

The same can be said for courage, as leading requires you to make and execute hard decisions, to tell people things they don't want to hear (e.g., the truth). Leadership roles typically involve taking a higher degree of career risk. Put simply, your job is less secure. It comes with the territory.

Competence is found in deeds more so than just words. Sadly, some folks are put into leadership roles without it. We have many incompetent people in major leadership positions today and the worst part is that they don't realize their incompetence (nearly everyone else does), and it's not altogether their fault.

Too often, when a first-line leadership role opens, management, in its infinite wisdom, goes to the longest serving non-management employee and tells them that they're moving up, starting next week, and they've got all weekend to get ready. Never mind whether they even want the job or think they're ready for it.

> "All of us have the spark of leadership in us, whether it is in business, government, or as a nonprofit volunteer. The challenge is to understand ourselves well enough to discover where we can use our leadership gifts to serve others. We're here for something. Life is about giving and living fully."
>
> Ann Fudge, CEO - Young & Rubicam

One of the most outstanding leaders in my lifetime, Murray Lynn was both a hero in life, and someone whose legacy will positively influence the world forever! Murray Lynn was an outstanding human being, leader, and world influencer, a true hero in every sense.

He was born as Moshe Leicht, to Rosa and Abraham Leicht, in Bilke, Hungary. Tragically in 1942, Murray's dad was killed by the Arrow Cross fascists, Hungarian counterparts to German Nazis.

In April of 1944, the deportation of over 800,000 of Hungary's Jews began, when the Arrow Cross forced families from their homes to the train station. After spending a few days in a ghetto, Murray, his three brothers, and his Mother were crammed into a cattle car with other Jews and sent to Auschwitz.

Their journey took 72 hours with no stops and no food. His mother and brothers were murdered upon arriving in Auschwitz. Murray survived the concentration camp, despite unbearable conditions and a death march that lasted many weeks.

As an orphaned teenager, he was sent to England, Ireland, and ultimately America, where he began a new life. In New York, Murray worked his way through college, graduating from Bernard Baruch College. Working many early jobs in sales, he rose to lead several successful businesses in the chemical industry, settling in Atlanta, and marrying Sonia, the love of his life.

Murray was in his 60s before he could speak to those outside the family about his Holocaust experience. Once he did, he spoke to large groups of all ages, ethnicities, and races throughout the world, spreading his message of love, resilience, forgiveness, and determination with an overriding objective of educating people on the horrors of hate, bigotry, discrimination, and prejudice.

His desire was to prevent further occurrences of this sort through education.

I've never known a person with as much humility, courage, strength, and unselfishness as Murray Lynn. As a true victim physically, emotionally, and in ways unimaginable to civilized humans, Murray never succumbed to victimhood. With forgiveness for his tormentors, he sought a world of peace, civility, love, and understanding.

In 2015, The Bremen Museum produced a video, **Unconquered: Murray Lynn**, narrated by former Atlanta Mayor and United Nations Ambassador,

Andrew Young. You may watch it via YouTube at: https://www.youtube.com/watch?v=Ef3c8U2lgVo. It's 37 minutes long, well-worth the time, and a riveting lesson on this horrible chapter of world history.

A special friend to me, he was a wonderfully authentic role model whose strong leadership and positivity made a real difference on Earth!

So much that happens or doesn't happen in the organizational world stems from trust. One of the root enabling factors for trust is the belief that the person to be trusted is sufficiently competent to perform should they choose to. As a case in point, prospective employees are told every day by hiring managers that "We firmly believe in developing talent, and I will make it my business to see that you're prepared for the next thing up the line." Never mind the solemnity of their intentions, too many of those people wouldn't know where to start or wouldn't recognize a good development program if their life depended on it.

In a webinar on Leading In a Crisis done in April, 2021 for WAPOlive, New Hampshire Governor, Chris Sununu crisply made the point that "trust stems from transparency." It is incumbent on leaders at every level to be who they say they are.

WHAT?

1. People who look to us in a leadership role have a right to expect that first and foremost, we are a reasonably competent, well-adjusted adult human being who is comfortable in their own skin, capable of playing nice with, and being considerate of others.
2. They also have a right to expect us to demonstrate high standards, low tolerance for misfits, good levels of judgment, discretion, fairness, and listening.
3. Transparency is an essential requirement of trust.

SO WHAT?

1. It's important for us to realize that more people quit their boss than their job, and they generally quit their boss first.
2. Triumph and good example can arise from hardship, witness Murray Lynn.
3. "Soft skills" done poorly, get hard real fast.

NOW WHAT?

1. No matter how technically/operationally skilled or talented they may be, we should refrain from putting anyone in a leadership role who lacks understanding of what they are getting into, and the requisite unteachable qualities (e.g., courage, character, curiosity, humility, thick skin, bias for action, common sense.)

Chapter 6:
COURAGE
(When the Bear's Hungry, and You're Handy)

"Being responsible sometimes means pissing people off."

Gen. Colin Powell, US Army (ret.)

Leadership involves having the courage to take risks, tell people the unvarnished truth, make tough values-based decisions, even in a headwind when everyone, (including you) is scared. I'll go out on a limb and suggest that this is another of the short list of leadership characteristics that are basically unteachable, and nature trumps nurture.

Leadership often entails dealing with tough and unpleasant decisions. Sometimes the alternatives are ugly. The greater good will usually prevail when leaders have the fiber to choose the best from among no perfect options. Done well, being a leader is not a popularity contest. It's about regularly doing the right thing at the right times, even when it's unpopular. It's about mutual respect…earning it and giving it. Strong leaders have the ability, the responsibility, and the willingness to make the hard calls when they are needed.

Moral courage is the ability to admit mistakes and make tough choices in the face of criticism. Great leaders always base their courage on the conviction of their values. Moral courage is not about getting the most votes or winning a popularity contest; it's about having a reputation for doing what's right and best under the circumstances.

A Missile Gone Wrong

In September 2021 as US military forces were completing their exit from Afghanistan under near constant threat of attack, detection of a terrorist bombing plot against those forces was discovered. After eight hours of observation via overhead air assets, a white Toyota vehicle believed to be transporting explosives instrumental in the plot was destroyed via a remotely controlled Hellfire missile. It was initially reported that the missile had successfully found and destroyed the vehicle, killing the occupants.

Days later, on or about September 17, US CentCom Commander, General Kenneth McKenzie appeared on global television news coverage with obvious pain on his face and announced that, in the fog of war, his troops had erred in targeting the vehicle and mistakenly killed ten members of an Afghan family, including seven children. His remarks were completed with an unambiguous apology, repeated for emphasis.

Saying "No"

In what is by far his most popular song, rock artist, Meatloaf says, *"I'll do anything for love, but I won't do that."* Our success as leaders is heavily dependent on our willingness and ability to say, no, I won't do that. But unlike Meatloaf, we must be clear about what "that" is. I won't put that item on my plate, as it's inconsistent with the priorities I have been given and accepted. No, that's not good enough. No, you can't do that and continue working here, and the list goes on. And speaking of plates, it's reported that the one thing that won't be taken from Meat's plate is his favorite post-gig treat, P.F. Chang lettuce wraps.

Saying no is not a matter of being mean, difficult, argumentative, or confrontational, but being clear. In fact, the better leaders I've had the pleasure to be around have in their own way, found ways to say no and be helpful at the same time, e.g., I can't help you with that, but let's see if I can find someone who can. Or, my schedule simply doesn't permit my attending that meeting next Thursday. I'm happy to take fifteen minutes right now and discuss it with you if it would be of help. In other words, where possible, they look for a way to say, "No, but…" At the other end of the same pew, they also look for opportunities to say, "Yes, and…" further sweetening an affirmative answer with what the Creole refer to as lagniappe, a "little something extra."

Too, we must have the courage to make, announce, and stand behind unpopular decisions, even those that you may not be able to fully explain at the moment, or even agree with. Sometimes, often in fact, it is the leader's duty to salute and execute no matter their feelings. You better be able to explain a decision though before you ask the team to execute it. "Here's what, here's why, any questions? Let's talk about how and when."

Do this "because I said so, because I'm the boss and you're not" never did work very well. It certainly doesn't today, when everyone has at their fingertips the means to gather data on their own and to actively oppose a decision that appears half-baked. The bad news is that courage at this level is generally something that cannot be taught. It's factory installed. You either have it in sufficient supply and are willing to use it, or you don't. The lack of sufficient courage doesn't make someone a bad person, but it does (or should) disqualify them from leadership as an avocation.

When You've Screwed Up

Upon discovering that you've made a mistake, courage also means saying, "This One's on Me." I messed up. Doing so is essential to building trust, and a hallmark of great leaders. In an October 2021 appearance before Netflix workers who were upset by an offensive rant from comedian Dave Chappelle, CEO, Ted Sarandos did exactly that, plainly announcing, "I screwed up…"

*"You will never do anything in this world without courage.
It is the greatest quality of the mind next to honor."*

—Aristotle

Leadership Choices – Slices of the Pie

We hear from others about getting their "fair" share. Sometimes folks are so intent on protecting their turf — their slice of the pie — that they forget why they have that "slice" in the first place. If the size of the pie is fixed, playing a "zero sum" game and giving a larger slice to one party necessarily means reducing the size of other slices. In any organization, bickering, jealousy, and internal strife can sometimes overshadow performance and undermine goals. Good, mature leaders are willing to Jaywalk a bit to see if perhaps the pie can be expanded.

When turf wars inevitably break out, leaders need to rally their staff to work in harmony to make the pie bigger, so everyone receives a larger piece, or so another person can be added and yet no slices are reduced in size. It amazes me that some folks want to fight internally rather than focus their efforts on the competition, the guys and gals on the other side of the field who would take food, every bite of it, out of the mouths of your babies… the real entity needing their full attention. Sometimes I wish we had different uniforms from our competitors, much like sports teams, so energies were better spent beating the other team, not the friendlies.

Most teams in fact perform better with a declared "enemy." We just need to make sure it's not the folks in our same locker room. Indeed, FedEx founder Fred Smith once declared in an interview that, "If UPS hadn't come along, we would have had to invent them. We're so much better for having the competition." Sears might have done better to have taken the same approach with Walmart and Amazon.

Reward Performers

Not long ago, a leader talked with me about the notion of uniformly giving 2% (non-COL) pay increases to everyone in their organization, in lieu of using any merit-based differentiation. "Why on Earth would you want to do that", I asked. It could be a sure way to lose the best performers, keep the mediocre ones, and perhaps worst of all, to reward those whose next job you really hoped would be with a competitor.

Sadly, too many organizations, some that you know the names of, are doing exactly that. They've stopped doing any work performance appraisals, too (because they require courage and copious amounts of time), and strangely, they are wondering why they're having so much difficulty finding and keeping good people. Simple - good performers don't want to work with or be rewarded like turkeys.

Failure to differentiate and appropriately reward performance will create a culture that brings the entire organization down to its lowest common denominator. The most capable (and employable) people tend to have the greatest opportunity to leave, and if not appreciated, with money, career growth, and other forms of recognition, they'll exercise that prerogative. Moreover, their exit will be hastened by the fact that they are tired of carrying other people's water. Any organization that fails to notice and differentiate performance does so at its peril.

Involving others in the slicing of the pie is often productive. When my children were small, heated debates would often occur whenever cake or pie was to be sliced into portions for each of them. After more unsuccessful schemes than I can count, I stumbled on a simple solution where we let one cut the cake, and the other to choose their slice. Suffice it to say the routine of cake slicing went from seconds to minutes. God forbid that your brother or sister got a slice even one nanometer larger than yours. Involving your folks in the division of the team's pie will not only improve fairness, but you will gain terrific information on how well values are aligned.

Dealing With Problematic People

Part of every leader's job involves dealing with people who are not behaving or performing acceptably. Quite often the first person we have to deal with in such cases is ourselves. Nobody likes problems, and we can easily find a hundred more fun things to do than to sit down with someone and have what could be a difficult conversation.

But having the conversation comes with the territory, and truth be known, we've probably not exactly been set up for success by getting any training or doing any reading up on managerial coaching. Should you choose to do the latter, I highly recommend one of my favorites, *The Coach*, a book by Starcevich and Stowell. It offers an 8-step coaching model that actually works. Nothing new or sexy, it's simple as dirt, and effective.

A Few Working Principles To Guide You:

- Don't ignore performance or behavioral issues - They seldom self-correct, and instead, usually grow over time, forcing a harder discussion later.
- Whatever the issue is, be willing to discuss it from both your and the other person's perspective (for real).
- Be willing to own ways in which you bear partial (or even total) responsibility for the matter e.g., miscommunication, lack of training, poor support…
- Help the other person see the impact that the matter is having on them, customers, fellow employees, etc. Whenever possible, look for the personal impact.
- Pursue reasonable solutions. When possible, incorporate their ideas. Make it a "we plan."
- Agree to proceed, with clear steps, goals, & timetables. Get Commitment (capital "C' intentional).
- Follow up - Be quick to recognize progress. The sooner you can notice real progress being made and reinforce it, the better.

"You Can't Always Get What You Want"

Making a critical point on choices and differentiation, The Rolling Stones, on their 1969 *"Let it Bleed"* album, released the hit song, *"You Can't Always Get What You Want"* with the headline lyrics: "You can't always get what you want, but if you try, sometime, you find, you get what you need."

Our world today makes choices about how to divide the pie every day. The city of Detroit declared Chapter 9 bankruptcy in 2013 all because everyone wanted a bigger piece of the pie. After trying mightily to give people everything they wanted, the city ran out of cash (surprise!), found itself with billions of dollars of debt, and no ability to repay it.

We all know the saying: "You can't have your cake (or pie) and eat it too." One of my pet peeves is seeing our national and civic leaders ignore this fact. They tell voters they can have things for "free" while ignoring the fact that someone must pay for these things. If no one can, the whole country will end up like Detroit.

As our government doles out shares of the pie with no concern for who earns it, the good businesses — and the good jobs — will leave the country and go where they are more highly valued the same way that talented, productive employees will leave a company that does not give them what they earn.

"Pie Chart of Life"

Another interesting concept involving pies is what I call the "Pie Chart of Life." Simply put, we can imagine our lives, our weeks, days, and hours as pie charts with the beginning and the end of each encompassing the "pie." In life all of us are involved in many activities: Business, family, religion, civic activities, recreation, fitness, children's activities, etc.

As outstanding as some people are, it's virtually impossible to excel at everything. Correction, it is impossible. There are tradeoffs, relative strengths, and weaknesses if you will. You might be an "A" in family and children's activities but just a "B" in business and perhaps a "C" in civic and church activities. And maybe you neglect your fitness, health, and sleep pretty much altogether resulting in a "D" or "F" in those.

We have choices in how we make the trade-offs, and those selections affect your success and happiness. Aligning those decisions with the values and things that are most important to you will make the trade-offs far easier and will lead you to greater satisfaction with your choices and stronger relationships with those whom you share mutual values.

Your Life as a "Pie" - Always Being Baked

What I mean is this: Consider your life as a pie in progress. Each of our lives carries a different recipe and our ingredients change over time. No two people are identical.

In the beginning our ingredients are parents, teachers, ministers, coaches, neighbors, and friends — they give us the knowledge and values that help make us who we are. As we grow up, we have the opportunity to choose our own ingredients. Our pie is never fully baked until our final breath so we should try to improve the recipe every single day. Start today: Choose to enrich your ingredients and choose to be a powerful ingredient for others.

WHAT?

1. Like a handful of the other characteristics dealt with in this book, courage is also factory-installed. I've seldom, if ever seen it added once the pie is baked.
2. Good leaders look continually for ways to expand the pie.
3. One of the hardest things that leaders must do, at any level, is to turn off their felt need for popularity and say "no."

SO WHAT?

1. Developing a reservoir of good coaching methods and habits builds confidence, which reduces the intensity and repetitive nature of potentially confrontational situations.
2. Leaders lacking in courage and coaching skill tend to use more power than necessary to control potentially contentious conversations.

NOW WHAT?

1. Make it a point to develop your coaching skills, and use them.
2. In hiring people for leadership roles, use behaviorally anchored interview questions to identify those with sufficient courage to lead.

Chapter 7:
CURIOSITY
(Lack of it killed the cat)

"Curiosity is one of the central traits I look for when hiring, for any position. Curious individuals often come up with the most innovative and even breakthrough ideas that can make a real difference in business. Curious people probe and ask the questions that can make some leaders feel a little uncomfortable. And that's OK, too. My attitude is, bring it on! We need thought-provoking team players who challenge the status quo."

Joe Scarlett - Chairman (ret.) Tractor Supply Corp.

Great leaders have inquisitive minds. They are continuous learners, always seeking to better themselves mentally and professionally. They are full of questions and genuinely want to hear what others think, and see what they see. It is from this collective wisdom that they build consensus and sound direction. Egotistical know-it-alls will never be leaders in the truest sense because of their unwillingness to listen to others, consider fresh perspectives, think deeply, introspectively, to evolve.

Ask More & Better Questions

Suggesting perhaps that as leaders we don't have the market cornered on brains and good ideas, former Tractor Supply Corp. Chairman & CEO Joe Scarlett suggests that there are clear benefits to taking interest in the knowledge and opinions of others…"It sounds silly, but being curious makes you a smarter, more interesting person. When you can ask good questions and show genuine interest in others' lives, people will gravitate toward you." https://joescarlett.com/leadership/why-dont-you-ask-more-questions/

Curious leaders, equipped with inquisitive minds are given to wonder, What if? Why? Why not? They tend to ask more questions, better questions, because they're curious, and willing to be a little bit naive… Always seeking knowledge and understanding.

Willing to step outside the crosswalk, they go where the answers, the real nuggets are likely to be, and are unafraid to learn from people 40 years or 14 pay grades their junior, or senior, as the case may be. Striving for both personal and professional competence, they are happy to meet with the folks where the rubber meets the road, learn from the grass roots, from the field: Customers, employees, vendors, competitors, industry, the Lyft driver. Whoever, wherever, whenever.

"Oprah said that her critical skill as an interviewer was listening to what the interviewee was actually saying, and trying to understand the impact of what was being said. I have tried that approach to the best of my own ability. But Oprah has always had a unique way of showing empathy for her interviewees and audience, and it's that ability to connect so viscerally with those watching that has made her so appealing, so unique, and so influential."

David Rubinstein

What I hear David Rubinstein saying about Oprah is that having done her homework, (she's usually the most prepared person in the room), to include being prepared to ask good questions and then prepared to listen, really listen (and there's a profound difference.)

The top-down, highly directive, authoritative (I'm the boss and you're not) management style from our past doesn't work anymore. Truth be known, it never did, if only for the obviously flawed logic behind the assumption that leaders knew everything, or at least always knew best. People simply tolerated it, to our faces. In its place, today we find far less arrogant, more collaborative leaders whose technique matches up better with a workforce that has an informed opinion and wants to express it. They want to be heard. No, it's stronger than want… They demand to be heard.

Our Duty to Learn/Grow

Another clear demarcation is the transition from a mindset where in the past, once anointed a manager, you became all knowing, infallible, and exempt from further learning, beyond what you might gather from reading the WSJ. That has changed, a lot. For openers, what's a newspaper? ☺

> *"Humility. It's really important to know what you don't know and listen to people who do know what you don't know."*
>
> George W. Bush to David Rubinstein,
> on what it takes to be President

As CEO of PepsiCo, Indra Nooyi made the tough decision to overhaul Pepsi's IT systems. To understand the needs, technologies, and possibilities, over a holiday period she read a stack of textbooks cover to cover and had professors on call for private tutoring. This level of preparation did much more than inform her choices, it enabled Ms. Nooyi to convince doubtful skeptics through reason rather than brute force to sign on to the change. As noted by Ruth Umoh, Ms. Nooyi offered a lesson for the rest of us… "When you have a competence that nobody else has, you become more valuable." https://www.cnbc.com/2018/10/02/pepsico-ceo-indra-nooyis-last-day-5-habits-that-drove-her-success.html

Growth mindset. Never a victim. Ask yourself at the end of each day: What were my wins/accomplishments? My losses or missed opportunities? What did I learn? What got away from me? What am I going to repeat, and conversely, what am I going to do better tomorrow?

As the pace of change in our world continues to advance, we simply don't have the time to absorb new data and understanding at a rate that was sufficient 20 or even 5 years ago. Our children are learning things in the 3rd grade many of us didn't get until high school, if at all. Witness not just the ability to operate a micro-computer, but the ability to make it do real work, and answer questions for us.

Stepping into the way back machine for a moment, at the age of ten, I wasn't trusted or allowed to pick up the receiver of our family's rotary-dial, party-line telephone (hello?) and make or even answer a call unsupervised, for fear that I might make a "long distance" call and incur toll charges our family couldn't afford.

By comparison, just this week, I casually observed a home-schooled four-year-old girl initiate a FaceTime call via her Mom's cell phone with a grandparent 900 miles away, all by herself. Her nine-year-old brother, who was miffed because little sister was monopolizing the phone figured out on his own how to get a Skype account and begin initiating calls with friends from his iPad. He did it within about five minutes. He has also learned that, until recently, he could log onto Amazon, order all kinds of neat stuff without putting up any money of his own, and so long as he could hide the newly delivered stuff before his parents found out, it was a nifty deal. If we're failing to keep up with the pace of learning, we are being left behind with that rotary dialed phone, and less money.

My sense is that we materially underestimate the beneficial power of curiosity. If nothing else, it causes us to slow our pace of thinking for a bit while we sort out new possibilities. We learn to better appreciate the views and ideas of people around us who are helping us create a mosaic. By making some changes to the boxes on our org charts, as Indra Nooyi was encouraged by Steve Jobs to do, we open new relationships and possibilities.

It's important (no, vital) that we find out even before making a hiring decision, not just what prospective teammates need to learn, but how they learn best. What learning style works best for them? Are they a reader, a visual learner (think YouTube), or do they prefer a concrete experience? It matters, a lot.

People who know a lot more about the matter than I do suggest that there are a variety of distinctly different adult learning styles, and that it behooves us to shape learning content and delivery to suit those style preferences. One size fits a few, not most. Will their learning pace be sufficient in the new environment? Do we have the capability to help them learn the things that will be instrumental to success? If not, take a pass rather than frustrate them and their new coworkers. I'm serious about this. A mismatch of learning styles is as important as a mismatch of values.

More important even than the efforts we take to assist in the development of those around us are the steps and habits we employ to keep ourselves learning, growing, and relevant. People who are slow to ingest new data and react to it have no business venturing out into traffic, let alone Jaywalking.

In a September 19, 2020 WSJ piece referencing what he has termed "Huang's Law," named for Nvidia founder, Jensen Huang, author Christopher Mims describes how the silicon chips that power AI more than double every two years. Although it's hard to imagine still smaller and faster microchips, futurists suggest that our progress will advance 20,000 years (comparatively) in just the 21st century alone.

Developments in AI, robotics, cognitive sciences, nanotechnology, neuroscience, energy, and medicine will change our lives in ways we can barely imagine. In our lifetime, kidneys and livers that are now being made experimentally will likely be produced on 3-D printers and transplanted into human patients, saving hundreds of lives weekly, and $billions. In the meantime, as an aside, if you're not already a designated organ donor, please thoughtfully consider it.

Repetitive (human) tasks will continue to be automated, simplified, and tasked to machines and software. An ever-increasing amount of information will be available, and machine sorted almost instantly. The good news for us is that a premium will be placed on key skills best done by real, pulsating humans—especially critical thinking.

Following are some things we all need to do to survive and thrive during this time:

Don't Chase Parked Cars

Dogs don't do it, and neither should you. We simply must keep moving and learning throughout our careers, and our lives beyond the career stage. It's in our best interest to build a reservoir of personal intellectual property, and to leverage our value via curiosity. We have little choice but to become lifelong learners, never satisfied with the status quo. If you need any more impetus to do so, imagine spending the rest of your life as one who has become irrelevant, and is known as such. That scares the bejesus out of me, and it should you, too.

> "Life is a succession of lessons that must be lived to be understood."
>
> Helen Keller

We don't need all the answers, but let's keep asking great questions and reading/watching/absorbing everything we can with a voracious appetite, even in settings where learning seems less obvious. Take advantage of learning opportunities from a variety of sources, including the bountiful supply of webinars, Massive Open Online Courses (MOOCs), seminars, lectures (I LOVE those presented at New York's 92nd Street Y, aka 92Y), workshops, and videos—many of which are completely free. If you go in person to 92Y, plan to arrive an hour or so early so you can catch dinner at Sfoglia Restaurant across the street.

Similarly, there are an emerging set of certificate programs sponsored by well-respected organizations like Disney and Google. At the other end of the spectrum, we have a growing population of Baby Boomers who have earned those gray hairs by experiencing things that we haven't. Shown just a little respect, many of them are only too happy to pass along some of the lessons they've learned the hard way, so you don't have to. This is only the tip of the iceberg. Keep your eyes and ears open, very open.

> "If you don't like change, you'll like irrelevance even less."
>
> Gen. Eric Shinseki

Be Open To Change

Learning is more than an academic exercise. It can enable change, which is one of the few constants in life. To perform at our very best we must be willing and able to adapt. Consider the very real possibility that most of tomorrow's jobs don't even exist yet, and regardless of age, most of us will always have a job of some sort.

Skill/knowledge capabilities that landed primo jobs yesterday are currently being subsumed by AI (think accounting and law among them). The necessity of having a 4-year college degree for many occupations is being reconsidered, and while graduation is an accomplishment, it's but one step on the educational path to success and positive influence on others. Resting on your laurels or that twenty-year-old diploma never was a good idea, even less so today.

Dare To Be Unique

As humans, we have untapped reservoirs of thinking power and yet most of us use our brain potential all too sparingly. Our mindsets and belief systems can inhibit potential growth. Be willing to open your mind to new thinking while embracing growth mindsets with a willingness to value new information and see the opportunities that fresh insight brings. Be willing to see life and its many possibilities beyond the "zebra stripes" of the crosswalk. Practice asking, "What if… Why not?"

Seek Truth

In an age of instant information and social media we are often driven by sound bites and data wholly unsupported by fact or reliable research. Witness widespread use, beginning in 2017 by supposedly serious-minded people in real jobs, of what they termed "alternative facts." Operating at a frenetic pace, we're afraid to slow down long enough to review it in depth or probe for reasonableness. Yet, it is up to us to seek the truth, to question rigorously, to reach for deeper understanding, and recognize BS when we encounter it.

Never in history have we had the resources we now have to learn and think for ourselves. As leaders who are influencers and role models, we are responsible for separating the pepper from the fly poo (think about picnics, open food containers, and tiny black spots on the potato salad ☺) and furthering conversations in thoughtful ways. Brains used properly have vast memory power and can update their operating systems instantly (in far less time than it takes to update an iPhone) with new knowledge.

Develop Human Connections

In a world of virtually limitless digital connectivity, it is vital that we strive to develop and meaningfully grow our human connections, with emphasis on "meaningfully." The person with the most Twitter followers or Facebook "friends" is not declared the winner.

Developing emotional intelligence while balancing empathy with logic will be at a premium in the very near future. It's not an either/or proposition. Being masterful at the things only humans can do best will serve us well. Interpersonal relationships, understanding behavior, and being adept at making decisions based on human understanding and cold logic will be huge assets.

> "Your legacy is every life that you've touched. We like to think that these great, philanthropic moments are the ones that leave the impact, or will make the huge difference in the world, but it's really what you do every day. It's how you use your life to be a light to someone else's."
>
> Oprah

Bridge Generational Divides

Generationally, we have many different value systems and attitudes in play in today's workspace, ranging from Boomers to Millennials to Gen Z. Like it or not, we filter much of what we observe and hear through our generational experience filters and tend to shape our observations to reinforce our beliefs and biases.

That can be problematic, as it can jaundice our thinking. We tend to do better when we work collaboratively to understand one another and to improve, while reshaping our belief systems in congruence with new realities.

I strongly encourage you to get out of your comfort zone to do some of this. I am an unabashed user of the Apple store. This Boomer has learned a ton from the kids aka "geniuses" in those stores (and they are), but only when I'm willing to approach them on an even footing and not try to show them how smart I am. And yes, Tim Cook, I always leave smarter thanks to those geniuses, but usually with some new gear and a lighter wallet too.

Trust And Learn From Your Peers

By working openly with peers both inside and outside the organization you can create a trusting, confidential environment to make each other better. One good rule of thumb in networking is to pay it forward whenever you can. A small but significant way of doing so is to prioritize time with and for someone else's benefit. By approaching issues without agendas and each bringing their own unique experiences to bear, you create mutual benefit, win-win scenarios.

Find A Role Model, Mentor, Sponsor, Coach

In addition to insight that we're able to acquire on our own, success is dependent on learning from others. The pace of the game today is such that we need knowledgeable, agenda-free inputs from a variety of sources. Consider the fact that in the 2021 season, the reigning Major League Baseball champion Los Angeles Dodgers, with a 40-player roster, had no fewer than 13 coaches, with coaches for all positions and aspects of the game. Similarly, the reigning WNBA champion Seattle Storm has 12 players and 4 coaches plus a trainer. And you have how many professional coaches available to your team?

All of us have need of role models and mentors, and at times, coaches of our own. If you don't already have those folks on your team (personally and organizationally), get busy! That said, it's also your responsibility to be a mentor for others, and as a leader, it is your duty to be a role model and coach for those around you. It's a big (and growing) part of what, as a leader, you get paid to do.

By the way, this learning exchange isn't just a philanthropic exercise. Leaders who show serious interest in the development of staff earn valuable reputations as "talent magnets", which is a very bankable asset, one that appreciates over time and pays handsome dividends.

The pace of play today is such that if you're not constantly getting better, you're going backward, losing ground, losing competitiveness. Invest some time every day in developing yourself and those around you. Your return will be a lifetime of energetic contribution and personal growth, rewarding you with the sense of making a difference and maybe a championship or two along the way!

Professional development is as important for those in the C-suite as anyone else. In fact, it's more important. One of the first things Indra Nooyi did upon being appointed CEO at PepsiCo was to pay a visit to Steve Jobs who, according to Ms. Nooyi was quite generous with both his time and advice. One of the things Jobs strongly suggested to her was that, if a particular function or initiative was of key importance to her, it should report directly to her as a clear sign of the degree to which she prioritized it. Moreover, the more immediate relationship would likely accelerate her growth and awareness in that arena.

Similarly, explaining perhaps some of his own emotional outbursts, Jobs suggested that Ms. Nooyi be overtly demonstrative of her discomfort when something that was a high priority was going sideways. In other words, his reputation for being a little (okay, a lot) difficult and demanding at times wasn't always an accident. For what it's worth, Ms. Nooyi acknowledged that she had taken that advice to heart and found it often had the desired effect. One caveat in that regard: Don't ever single someone out and 'climb on their bumper' in public. They'll never forgive you, nor should they.

Leaders Use Mirrors To Grow

Leaders are often asked to consider a famous metaphor – that of "looking into the mirror" to evaluate honestly and objectively their strengths and challenges and to better find their growth paths as professionals. This self-assessment can help executives evaluate their impact on others as well as give them useful feedback as to their own self-development and future direction.

However, honestly evaluating oneself is no easy task; when objectivity and balance can be hard to come by. One role that I've played regularly as a CEO and executive coach is acting as a mirror for clients and teammates. To gain maximum benefit from that relationship, part of our deal must be an understanding that the "mirror doesn't always smile back." In providing candid, unfiltered feedback to the leader, a mentor or coach can be invaluable in helping leaders see themselves as they are, (or at least as they are perceived), as opposed to what their own self-image may be.

Perceptive leaders learn early on that the closer you get to the top, the harder you must work to get objective, no holds barred feedback, because power tends to evoke fear that corrupts people's feedback mechanisms. We may not want it to be that way, but it often is. And to be fair, some of us have a bad habit of "shooting the messenger." One organization that a lot of execs from small to mid-sized businesses turn to for this candor is Vistage, which offers a coaching and peer-peer advisory forum in most major markets.

We all have our imperfections — we don't need to self-evaluate to count all our weaknesses, yet it's important to remain ever mindful of the most important ones. We perform these necessary self-assessments to see what we can change about ourselves to be better as leaders, family members, and professionals. Life is about how we build on our experiences to grow, to be more fulfilled, and to bring happiness to ourselves and to others. Honest "reflection" can help each of us do just that.

In "Good to Great", Jim Collins uses a metaphor of windows and mirrors. "Great leaders" Collins says "look through the window when things go well" — that is they look at the team and give them credit. When things go poorly, they look in the mirror, evaluating themselves and taking responsibility for what went wrong so that they can fix it next time. Sadly, weak leaders do the reverse. They take credit and are inclined to engage in self-aggrandizement when things are rosy and blame their team or others when their train jumps off the tracks.

An ego-driven leader may be blinded by self-importance. That leader's team may become disengaged and feel unappreciated leading to defections, resentment, and failure to grow.

Self-Assessment and Difficult Feedback

The problem with looking in a mirror or performing an introspective self-evaluation is that it's difficult to judge oneself in a completely unbiased way. Just as physically you will never see yourself as others see you, so, too can it be difficult to realize how your actions affect others, and how they perceive you.

World-class athletes all have personal coaches. The best at their sports realize that an experienced professional can identify with clarity the things that they are doing well, and need to continue, and minor flaws that may be causing performance challenges. A truly independent and caring coach, mentor, or advisor will supercharge our personal development and growth as a leader.

As a "mirror that doesn't always smile back" my primary role is to be a truth teller.

When people look to me as a "mirror" to assess them, or the issues they bring to our peer group meetings, or me, they count on me to tell it like it is — honestly, objectively, and independently of their subjective wants or needs. Two conditions must exist before that relationship can proceed, however. First, the individual must believe that the coach is competent (there's that word again), that they know what they are doing before they start tinkering with someone else's career skills, and secondly, that they will have their client's best interest at heart, no matter what.

One tactic I've discovered and frequently employ before giving critical, let alone harsh feedback is to first ask permission to do so. Yes, permission. I do this regardless of our respective rank or position. I will often frame the feedback agreement this way: "I think I'm seeing something that may be keeping you from being as successful as you would like. Would you like to hear about it?" I ask the question, shut up, and let them answer, and "no" is usually an acceptable answer.

Nearly always, the answer is yes, which gives me a green light to proceed, and obligates them to listen and at least consider the feedback as a gift, in the manner intended.

I will never forget doing so one time with a bristly guy with a big ego two levels my senior in the organization where I then worked, who answered in the affirmative, but then added, "as long as you keep in mind the difference between feedback and insubordination." Being something of a smart-mouth, I asked him, with a slight grin on my face, to kindly alert me two nanoseconds before I was in danger of crossing that line. It went down fine.

By helping people see themselves as they really are, we're energizing them to become the person and leader they have the potential to be. Third-party opinions from respected advisors can help us all gain unbiased and fair perspectives of our strengths, weaknesses, and opportunities. It provides us a roadmap to improvement and growth.

Sadly, very few of the executives I've worked with have received even a modicum of honest feedback about their strengths and (particularly) their weaknesses or blind spots.

In your own life I encourage you to look into the metaphorical leadership mirror daily: Take stock of your actions and attitudes, and try to find a balance as you evaluate the day's successes and failures. The "mirror" helps us commit to continuous personal growth – starting from a foundation of accurately understanding ourselves, and clearly seeing where and how we can improve.

If you want to add to that, consider working with a coach, creating your own advisory board, or if at the CEO or any leadership level, becoming a member of Vistage.

WHAT?

1. Authoritarian leaders have long favored compliance over curiosity for obvious reasons. They don't want alternative thinking because they want to do all the thinking themselves and have people around them simply do as they're told. The worm has turned.

2. As professionals, we have a duty to learn and grow, and a need to do it faster than we're likely accustomed to.

3. Understanding the learning needs and styles of potential team members is vital.

SO WHAT?

1. We can often speed (and smoothen) the feedback process by asking permission to level with the other person. Can you stand some feedback?

2. When on the receiving end, we should treat well-intentioned feedback as a gift, whether we agree with it or not. Thank the person for it, and seriously consider it.

NOW WHAT?

1. Former Tractor Supply Corp. Chairman & CEO, Joe Scarlett made it a habit to look for innate curiosity in those he hired. You should, too, especially for leadership roles. Curiosity invokes "what if" thinking and enables higher order Strategic Jaywalking.

2. We all (especially at senior levels) need a mirror that has our best interests at heart and "doesn't always smile back." Make it happen via a coach or peer group. (Your boss likely isn't going to do it.)

3. As Indra Nooyi did with Steve Jobs, (and Vistage members do regularly), make good use of your peer groups, remaining mindful though that it's not a one-way street. Be prepared to pay it forward.

4. Take pains to ascertain the preferred learning style of potential teammates, before you commit to them.

Chapter 8:
JUDGMENT
(Coming in from the rain)

Good leaders uniformly evidence a rational thought process, mechanically sound methods for assessing a situation, examining risk/opportunity, weighing possibilities and options, gathering input/data, and pulling the trigger. Assessing the potential for Jaywalking is always in their playbook.

As importantly, they also have a knack for realizing when a fire should be left to burn itself out, a supposed dilemma is a non-issue, and that it really doesn't matter which of the available options is taken. In those cases, they are happy to delegate the matter or just let nature take its course. Realizing that every single event that crosses the horizon doesn't require or deserve the leader's attention saves them gobs of time and wear and tear on the people around them, who have better things to do than go on a low or no-yield adventure, aka a snipe hunt.

Good leaders are well aware of their core competencies and thus those areas where they can reasonably make judgment calls rather quickly, with an acceptable 'batting average' without a lot of added input. Yet they are also aware of the areas that are not their core strength and have the discipline and good sense to enhance their judgment by consulting other sources, and maybe staying a little closer to the signal light and crosswalks. Similarly, they take full advantage of the opportunities to expand their capability whenever possible through active learning.

One of the primary displays of a leader's judgment is in the caliber of people they surround themselves with. Good leaders tend to operate both with better process and more skill in the recruitment and selection realm. They don't wing it in this arena, preferring instead to methodically move through an examination and consideration process that affords both parties a good look at one another, and thus the chance to make better decisions. The proof is usually in the pudding.

Three suggestions I would make to you in this realm are:

1. Do an honest assessment complete with letter grade of your judgment (just judgment, not overall performance) in the following topical areas: Choice of Relationships, both personal and professional; Career Choices; Health & Wellness Choices; Financial Choices. If you're like me, you've got an uneven array of relative strengths. Then, ask yourself two sub-questions: Which judgmental strength should I be capitalizing more on, and which, given the chance, would I like to improve upon? Then, identify one or two people in your close network whose judgment you admire in these areas, and ask them for a conversation where they might share a tip or two. I think you'll be pleasantly surprised, possibly amazed.

2. To the extent that you decide to take some affirmative steps because of the foregoing analysis, find someone who will help support that effort: A coach, mentor, a Vistage chair, an executive assistant, or good friend…Someone who cares about you, who will listen, keep confidence, and occasionally ask a few hard questions to hold you accountable.

3. As you take affirmative steps to strengthen your judgment and decision making, give yourself some small rewards for the effort. You've earned it.

WHAT?

1. This is an area where leaders need to be self-aware, to know their strengths and shortcomings.

2. Given our paid responsibility to make decisions, it behooves us to have a logical decision-making process to rely on.

SO WHAT?

1. Too often, we hold decision-making responsibility a bit too tightly, and miss opportunities to further develop our teammates. The result can be direct reports who don't develop as quickly as you or they might like. Either condition will penalize you both.

2. Thoughtful analysis of the impact of a leader's judgment brings us quickly to hiring and firing decisions, where wins and losses carry significant consequence. The difference between a good and bad hiring decision, for example, cannot be overstated, ergo it makes considerable sense to spend quality time improving our batting average on such matters.

NOW WHAT?

1. One of the best things we can do for our judgment is to be constantly learning. Thankfully, our opportunities to do so are better than they've ever been. Use them. Think MOOCS, webinars, and private coaches.

2. Consciously defer some of the decision making to people junior to you, both as a developmental tool for them AND a time saver for you.

3. As you task others with higher order responsibilities, take pains to remind them that you're delegating partially for purposes of their development, that you remain available to them for consult, and that as long as they are behaving responsibly, doing what they genuinely believe to be right, no harm is going to come to them should things not turn out quite right.

Chapter 9:
CHARACTER
(Having it, not being it)

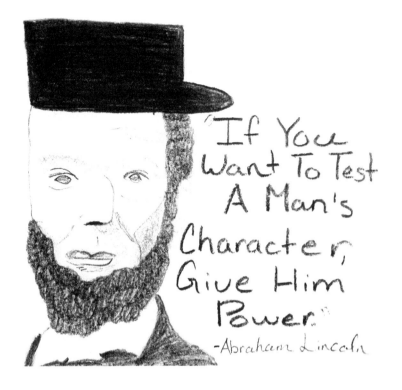

"If You Want To Test A Man's Character, Give Him Power."
-Abraham Lincoln

"Integrity is the soul of leadership!
Trust is the engine of leadership!"

— Amine A. Ayad

Authenticity is fundamental to character. What you see is what you get! No pretense or phony narratives. With the best leaders, you always know where they stand (and where you stand). Openness, candor, and clarity are their hallmarks. They listen well, while sharing their own candid thoughts. In a world seemingly dominated by fake, well, uh everything, that's truly refreshing.

Thinking back on the good leadership teams I've had the pleasure to associate with, one common factor was that there was no tolerance for games, politics, ulterior motives, excess political correctness, or outsized egos. Everyone knows what's going on and why. No hiding the ball. No room for secrets, backroom deals, or for being disingenuous. In each case, the sincerity of the leader fostered a transparent and inclusive culture. More, much more, (and better) work got done because they cut through the stuff.

They're for real. Straight shooters. The genuine article. Consistency. Again, my strong belief is that, after a certain stage in life, this is pretty much un-teachable. They tend to operate with a high degree of certainty about who and what they are, what they stand for, and stand means stand.

The mission they are on is an open book

In the movie "Brainpower," actor John Houseman, in his gravelly voice with a thick British accent recites the summary line of the movie, "You get what you expect to get. What are you expecting?" People who come to mind as some of the great leaders across time are very often not seen as the easiest folks in the world to work for or be around. They tend to expect a lot, both of themselves and the people around them. They hate losing in any circumstance, but the fear of losing by virtue of getting outworked makes them crazy.

Speaking about attorney and Atlanta Olympics ('96) organizer Billy Payne, friend Charlie Battle said, "He demands a lot of himself and others… Billy pushes people to try to get them to do things they may not think they can do."

Steve Jobs, co-inventor and former CEO of Apple, and Elon Musk of Tesla/SpaceX fame frequently get painted with the same brush. Some people maintain that those with extraordinarily high expectations, lots of power, and high intellect can, and do at times, cross the line and become unreasonable or even abusive. While I don't doubt the possibility of that occurring, I don't believe high expectations to necessarily be a causal factor.

Here's what I do know, though…

Houseman is right. We do tend to get what we expect (see "Pygmalion effect".) Those with modest expectations tend to get modest outcomes because they don't seem to dream quite as big, and that's what they are willing to settle for. I dare say that the Apple line of products and services from computers to tablets to music and the small devices with all their accoutrements would have nowhere near the brand stickiness and fan base f Steve Jobs had been willing to settle for something more Microsoftian, more pedestrian. (Sorry Mr. Gates, it's true. And yes, at one point, Bill Gates did save Apple from a pedestrian funeral with an infusion of cash.)

Over the years I have canvassed some of the people I know who worked directly for or near him via two questions: Did you ever "feel the heat" from him, and would you say that the experience of working around Steve Jobs, warts and all, made you better? The unequivocal answer in each case was, "absolutely."

Leaders of all stripes and stations in life are well advised to always have at least a couple folks around them who are unflinching truth tellers, people who care enough about them, who aren't put off by the power differential, and have the courage to come see you, close the door, sit down, and let you know that you have crossed a line, or are about to step in something that's not in your best interest.

Those people are worth their weight in gold because most others, due to the power differential, won't say anything. They'll see it, but they won't say it, to your face. We need to respect and appreciate those who care enough to take it a step further, because by virtue of their truth-telling, we're less likely to cross lines we shouldn't cross, and when we have, we have better opportunity to clean up our mess and make it right.

Good leaders tend to have sound moral compasses. Their honesty and values, seemingly from childhood reflect a deep sense of their purpose and the foundation of their decision-making. They don't need posters on the wall for others to know where they stand, but if they had one, it likely would be a picture of their Mother, who, more often than not provided the magnet for their compass. Each day they live and breathe their character.

It's not just their words but more importantly their deeds, their behavior that shows their true colors. They are predictable and are in pursuit of doing the right thing. Steadfastness of values creates a culture of integrity, attracting that same caliber of team members. And, it should go without saying, but the converse is also true. They will eject like a virus, those who prove lacking on this front. You should too.

WHAT?

1. In a word, authenticity is about being genuine, being who and what you say you are, irrespective of circumstances.

2. Character involves holding yourself and others to a higher standard, even (no, especially) when it's difficult or unpopular.

SO WHAT?

1. Authenticity can at times be made more difficult by the need for leaders to remain optimistic under virtually all circumstances. Not giddy, optimistic. I've long maintained that sometimes it is totally necessary to apply a little makeup to a pig, but not to the point that you're being deceitful about what animal is underneath the paint job.

2. For our teammates, living with an inauthentic or unprincipled leader is akin to trying to walk, let alone run with a shoe full of sand. It can only slow you down, and is certainly not conducive to Jaywalking.

NOW WHAT?

1. Given all the things that leaders have on their plate, it helps to have someone on the team or in your vicinity who cares enough to be a "mirror" as defined previously in this book, someone who will pull you aside and provide candid feedback (positive or otherwise) about your plans or behavior vs. espoused positions, and then forget that they ever had that little chat.

2. Be very careful, particularly as you ascend the leadership ladder not to become a little person with a little job and a big head.

3. Use the memory and teaching of your Mother to guide you in waters of temptation. What would she think or say about what you're about to do? If you can't think of how you might explain something to her, you probably should steer clear of it.

Chapter 10:
HUMILITY
(It's not all about whom?)

One of the very first things people are often struck with when in the company of a strong, successful leader is the unmistakable impression that it's NOT all about them. They aren't particularly impressed with their power, their responsibility, or stature. Rather, it's about the team and the mission, period.

They don't create a big, noisy wake as they go about their business, preferring instead to let their actions do the talking, and the team get the lion's share of any credit. I don't know if you can teach this. I'm inclined to say no, and willing to be wrong. I know who usually deserves much of the credit when it goes right… once again, Moms. They tend to be the ones who teach us manners, selflessness, how to share, and play nice in the sandbox.

Great leaders do not succumb to the lure of seeking ever more power, for the sake of having power. They are quite capable of saying, "No", "I don't need that', "I don't know", "I made a mistake", and "What do you think?"

They don't hog the spotlight or have a need to suck all the oxygen out of the room.

That said, let me part company with some traditional thinking which suggests that pride and confidence, seen as essential for those who would occupy leadership roles are somehow mutually exclusive of, and in essence the opposite of humility. I don't buy that for a second.

One of the largely unsaid (wink, wink, nod, nod) knocks on women in leadership roles is that they tend to be quieter, more reserved, less braggadocious, qualities that somehow get translated to lacking confidence, or a point of view, which couldn't be further from the truth. Speaking of truth, my strong suspicion is that notion emanates too often from a bro culture often clad in black t-shirts or Armani suits.

The ego can be one of the biggest barriers to success. Particularly for leaders who rely mainly on confidence, conviction, and self-assurance for effectiveness, an overactive ego can destroy collaborative effort, erode trust, and weaken morale faster than almost anything else.

Balancing self-confidence and humility while avoiding arrogance is the mark of a more fully formed adult and a true leader. I watch, listen, and talk with leaders for a living, and have done so for a long time. One of the first things I watch for is manners. Do they habitually hold a door for people? How do they treat flight attendants and restaurant servers? How do they treat the UPS driver? Does the word, 'please' seem comfortable leaving their lips? Are they noticeably listening to others, or merely waiting to resume talking?

You can spot it in their relationships and even their kids, e.g., I spoke a while back with someone who had spent the better part of three hours in the back of a corporate jet playing gin with the young, pre-teen son of an executive who was also on the plane. He was effusive in praising the kid's polite, responsive, self-effacing, manner, which just happened to mirror that of his Mom and dad who were sitting up front.

Curious, I asked about the kid's card playing. The quick and decisive answer was that he knew the game and was competitive as hell. He respected the age difference between he and his playing opponent, but proceeded to beat him like a drum at the game, smiled, and shook hands afterward, thanking the man for his company.

Accepting Responsibility Versus Giving Blame

Despite our best efforts, things occasionally go wrong. When they do, whether it's in the office or in the larger world around us, the tendency is to blame those in charge. "If he paid more attention" or "If she only had a better handle on things" then this or that would never have happened. There are nearly always other variables to consider in any event - and leaders who deservedly accept responsibility are that much closer to getting past the issue and moving on.

In some cases, assigning blame is necessary for accountability, but finger-pointing and shifting responsibility is never the answer. Some politicians do it regularly. In fact, that's about all they do. They can't wait to get in front of a camera and make someone else look bad. It's entertaining at times, but not a good look. Most won't complain, but they won't forget it either.

Giving Credit Versus Taking Credit

True leaders understand the value in giving credit for a job well done. Acknowledging when someone does something well is an easy way to build confidence and encourage desired behavior. Sharing credit with others in no way diminishes the leader who does so. It costs you nothing. It's not a zero-sum game.

Smart leaders know it feels good to be told you did a good job. Giving credit where it's due inspires others to reach for more of their best stuff on your behalf. Affirmation and acknowledgment foster trust and promote accountability. When employees see that leadership is aware of their efforts and recognizes when they do well, a partnership mentality develops where cohesive effort and collaboration thrive. Further, when they realize that you're being fair with them, they are more inclined to call it out when they've messed up, making the cleanup quicker and less messy.

Experienced leaders do more than give credit. Armed with deeper knowledge of the people around them, they make it a point to give recognition in the manner the individual prefers. Some people are delighted, for example, to get kudos in front of a crowd. As long as you pronounce their name right and give them a few moments with the mic, they're delighted. Others, not so much. More shy perhaps, they prefer that their appreciation come sans spotlight, in quieter, less public doses. It doesn't cost any more to recognize and show appreciation to them in the manner they desire. Moreover, they know darned well when you "do it their way," because you respect and care about them.

Avoiding Missed Opportunities

While leadership effectiveness demands a certain amount of technical expertise and know-how, the process is ongoing and there's never a point in time when any leader has got it all figured out. Indeed, here it is yet again. Good leaders have a fierce habit of being skilled, determined listeners. Witness another one of those people who can get away with only one name… Oprah, who, though for a long time was host of the world's greatest talk show, preferred to let her work (and not her mouth) do the talking. In a similar vein, she turned down more than one serious offer of support should she decide to run for President of the United States.

Take an hour and listen to a few of Oprah's interviews: e.g., w/ Elie Wiesel, Harry and Meghan, Mike Sisco, Whitney Houston… the list is long. More specifically than just 'doing' interviews, Oprah "gets people to talk" by being exceptionally well prepared and then approaching the subject out of curiosity on behalf of her audience, on their level. She gets more out of the interview because after posing a direct question with a smile (never a snarl), she lets them talk, during which she's actively listening, rather than figuring out what she's going to say next. It's about them, not her! Watch her and go to school on her!

Great leaders perceive their role as a journey, not an event. They embrace opportunities to improve and develop their skills. Building connections with people is much more than barking orders or even giving advice.

Roberto Goizueta, the Cuban-born immigrant who worked his way into the corner office of Coca-Cola was known as a learning executive by virtue of his willingness to freely admit his lack of knowledge on a subject, and pepper subordinates with questions to speed his learning. Similarly, he wasn't bashful about learning by taking business risks, not all of which turned out.

Extraordinary leaders get beyond expertise and impact those they work with on a personal and professional level. It's about helping others by giving back, by sharing wisdom with others to support, encourage, and inspire. Strong, confident leadership does not imply arrogance. The most effective eaders have learned the art of balancing self-assurance with listening skills, patience, continuous learning, and development.

When things are coming off the rails, good leaders are quick to examine their own behavior to see to what extent they might be contributing to the problem and hold themselves accountable first. That habit alone earns distinction for many as a talent magnet.

As noted in Roy Holley's book, *The Power of Moral Leadership*, "Those leaders who understand the law of stimulus and response understand that when they look in the mirror and change their own behavior to a higher plane, rather than first point a finger of blame, that change in stimulus will produce a different and higher response in others." Ding!

The real question is, what kind of leader do you want to be? Are you willing to share the stage with others? To give perhaps a little more credit and accept a little more blame than necessary? To be willing, like Roberto Goizueta to readily admit and then do something about knowledge shortfalls, OR to boastfully go through life and fake it till you make it, or not?

WHAT?

1. Leadership is not, repeat, NOT about you. Rather, it's about the team and the mission.
2. Humility and confidence are two unrelated traits, but for the fact that they are both qualities of a skilled leader and play nice together. Don't confuse humility with weakness or lack of confidence.
3. It's totally okay (no, necessary) to be the "boss" and still be seen as a learning professional.

SO WHAT?

1. Leaders who willingly accept an extra helping of responsibility when things go off the rails earn a different, higher response, and future benefit of the doubt from others.
2. You've got to decide what kind of leader you want to be, the one who operates largely through support, info sharing and encouragement, or the lone ranger.

NOW WHAT?

1. For a primer on how a true professional can make people feel good in their presence and attain their full cooperation, treat yourself to a half hour watching Oprah's interviews. You won't want to stop after thirty minutes.
2. Give serious thought to the kind of leader you want to be. Yes, you can choose, but you've gotta do the work.
3. Should you choose to make some changes in your leadership method, ask a peer, your boss, or coach to walk the first few steps with you. If you need a hand, don't be too proud to ask.
4. Okay, one more for the fellas… Stop quietly classifying your female counterparts as weak or indecisive because they're willing to listen and consider the input of others as a fundamental part of their operating process. You might instead watch and take a lesson.

PART 3:
Learned Leader Behaviors (Aftermarket)

Of the essential qualifications for leadership, some are more the product of nature, while others can be bolted on over time, through a process of nurture, or growth. Following is a description of the second cadre, the ones which are often developed through investment of time, effort, and sweat in the "aftermarket."

Chapter 11:
PRESENCE
(I'm supposed to be where?)

HANK
AARON

Known for his demeanor off the field
as much as his play on the field.

*"Leadership is about having the courage to be right
there with another person during their experience.
It's not about platitudes or scripted speeches, rather
the willingness to be there."* – Jennifer Tsang

Presence is a vital multi-dimensional aspect of leadership. First, it's a matter of choosing to be where you can do the most good and have the greatest impact in that moment.

Second, it's a matter of how you carry and comport yourself when you are "onstage" which is pretty much full time. It's a knack for showing up whenever and wherever your personal presence can make a difference - when people on the team are having a hard time, when the road is difficult, and the odds are long. Either personally or professionally.

What you say in those moments is almost immaterial. Rather, it's that you care enough to leave the comfort of your own surroundings to come be with your teammate(s) even if it's just for a moment, to let them know merely by your presence that they matter, and that you're thinking and caring about them. As an FYI, most of us are not good enough actors/actresses to fake it, so don't try.

In that sense, being present is an act of caring. Resultant from the 2020-21 pandemic, which put a heavy damper on travel and face-to-face (F2F) meetings, the physical grouping has, at times, been extremely difficult, yet I've seen some very good leaders go to extreme lengths to bridge the distance and send the message. Doing so means more now than ever.

Leaders Show Up

https://www.washingtonpost.com/lifestyle/2021/06/14/graduation-waffle-house-teen-work/

Writing for the *Washington Post* (6/14/21), Sydney Page chronicled the story of a young Alabama Waffle House employee who, on the day of his high school graduation, showed up to work rather than attending graduation, because his family was unable to accompany him, and truth be known, he likely couldn't afford the clothes to attend the ceremony. His Waffle House store manager, Cedric Hampton, wasn't having anything to do with that.

Long story short, following Hampton's lead, fellow employees and Waffle House patrons chipped in for some new clothes for the young man, took him shopping, got his graduation tickets, cap, gown, and drove him to the graduation site an hour away. They waited outside in the parking lot (due to Covid restrictions), while he attended the ceremony, walked the stage with his classmates, and received his diploma. *(Just stop for a few seconds and let that soak in.)*

By showing up, really showing up for one of his workers, Cedric Hampton left permanent marks on the young man, his teammates, and restaurant patrons alike about how leaders behave when the chips are down. I dare say none of them will forget his example, ever. I might also suggest that the restaurant patrons who witnessed or heard about the episode will likely continue their preference for waffles. Behaving as Cedric did is good for your reputation as a leader, an employer, and it's also good for business. A phrase I try to keep in mind is that it's behaviors that get results, not titles.

Long before Cedric was serving waffles, General Melvin Zais was a US Army General officer who served both in World War II and the Vietnam War. In a speech for the Delos C. Emmons Lecture Series at the Armed Forces Staff College, this tough, battle-hardened veteran talked not about tactics, weapons, or logistics but… are you ready for this? Caring.

Caring about the women and men with whom you work. A large part of the speech dealt specifically with the need for leaders to be physically present whenever people on their team are having a tough time and getting ready to do something even harder or more dangerous.

He specifically referenced situations in Vietnam when a helicopter crew was getting ready to go do a difficult extraction and they were sitting underneath the aircraft waiting, sweating, scared. He then talked about the fact that "You can smell fear in a person's breath, but you've got to get close enough to them to smell it. You don't have to say anything. They'll know that you know they're working like hell to make you look good." Presence.

In his Massachusetts-inspired accent, General Zais concluded his remarks as follows: *"I will ... provide you with ... the one piece of advice which I believe will contribute more to making you a better leader and commander, will provide you with greater happiness and self-esteem and at the same time advance your career more than any other advice which I can provide to you. And it doesn't call for a special personality, and it doesn't call for any certain chemistry. Any of you can do it. And that advice is that you must care."* As shown by Cedric Hampton, the general's advice is as applicable to civilians in the 2020's as it was soldiers in the latter half of the 20th century.

Hank Aaron

On January 22, 2021, the world lost a giant in the form of Major League Baseball star, Henry (Hammerin' Hank) Aaron, longtime star player with the Milwaukee and (later) Atlanta Braves. Aaron worked in a variety of assignments with the Braves after the conclusion of his playing days. He will forever remain a giant among all those even remotely familiar with the era in which he played professional baseball.

Aside from having retired as the MLB career leader in runs batted in (RBI), total bases, extra-base hits, and all-star appearances, along with being 2nd in home runs and 3rd in hits, Mr. Aaron is as well known for what he did off the field as on it. Specifically, having grown up in the deep South during segregation, Aaron carried the additional burden of being one of the very few Black superstar players in what at the time was an otherwise white sport, which preferred to stay that way.

With taunts and threats regularly directed toward him and his family, Aaron had the added distraction of constantly having to look over his shoulder. Yet, he didn't complain or make a public issue of it. As with every leader, Aaron quietly realized that by virtue of his stature, he carried the additional burden of high visibility and the need to constantly set a good example. In a statement shortly after Aaron's death, former President, Jimmy Carter said that "Henry Aaron became the first Black man for whom white fans in the South cheered."

As noted by Trinity Bland and Ryan Hardison in the *Daily Aztec*, *"Aaron was impressive in terms of having the most resilient, methodically productive career the world has ever seen, while also exuding a quiet confidence, resilience, and dignity, even when dealing with the sad reality of death threats as he approached Ruth's home run record."* The man transcended not just baseball, but Americana with grace, hope, class, and a rock-solid work ethic. Nobody outworked him.

Further measure of the man was taken in a game on April 4, 1974, when he hit the first pitch thrown to him by Cincinnati Reds pitcher Jack Billingham out of the park, thus tying the Major League Baseball home run record, until then held exclusively by Babe Ruth. "I never wanted them to forget Babe Ruth," Aaron said. "I just wanted them to remember Henry Aaron," proving that it takes no more energy or effort to win with class than without it... Just a wee bit more thought and consideration, of which we are all capable. Presence.

Soon thereafter, he broke Ruth's record with a towering shot into the bullpen at Atlanta Stadium, I was happy to be attending the game with my then nine-year-old son, Sean. It was a very special moment for us, too. Years later, quite by happenstance, I ran into him at a Little League game in Atlanta, where our sons were both playing. He mingled with the other parents, as any other normal guy, without an ounce of pretense.

> *"A leader's responsibility does not stop at the business door."* — Kat Cole

https://www.chicagoideas.com/videos/kat-cole-on-what-makes-a-leader

For decades, centuries perhaps, many business leaders have generally operated with clear demarcation between their business and personal lives, showing only a portion of their total self in each place. It's as if their coworkers and family each get half of a loaf, a different half. Many maintain that it's actually easier (less messy) that way, even though the burden of being one person at home and someone else in the workplace can grow tiresome. I know.

Truth be known it's a dirty little secret that really isn't much of a secret. Most of the people we interact with in the workspace (there is no more singular workPLACE anymore) realize, as do our friends and families that we're consciously leaving part of ourselves at the other place when we come home, or go to work. The folks at work likely wonder what the humanoid version of their leader is like, and I suspect many families choose to remain ignorant of what the warrior version of Mom or dad is all about.

During the time that I worked for a corporation away from home, I always chose to have at least a twenty-minute commute (usually more) between my two addresses so I could more comfortably make the mental shift while transitioning twice daily from one place (and personage) to the other. Of course, if you live near a major metropolitan area as I do, it doesn't take more than about five miles to get that buffer zone.

The COVID19 pandemic which made its way around the world and migrated to North America in early 2020 rearranged some of the aforementioned realities. Specifically, many of us found that, suddenly, those two different places (home and work) became one, as offices were closed, temporarily or otherwise, and working from home WFH (or elsewhere) became a fact of life for many.

> *"Being a woman is hard work."*
> — Maya Angelou

The slow, (too slow), but inexorable migration of women into the C-suite does more than break the glass ceiling. It serves to reduce this bifurcated personality, especially when Motherhood (In my book, Moms always get a capital M, because they deserve it) and management come together.

Speaking on the subject at the Women's Agenda Leadership Awards program (4/29/21), Angela Priestley opined… *"We saw the failures of a strongman style of leadership, of egos, of arrogance. Of those unwilling to listen to the science, unwilling to take decisive action. Unable to communicate and collaborate...*

"Much has been made of how female heads of state have led their countries during the pandemic — often to astounding success. Women lead a tiny 10% of countries, yet they've come out on top regarding Coronavirus responses. Jacinda Ardern in New Zealand, Tsai Ing-Wen in Taiwan, and Erna Solberg in Norway. They kept COVID cases and COVID-related deaths down."

Of those mentioned by Ms. Priestley, I can think of no leader who is doing a better job of displacing the dual role conundrum than New Zealand Prime Minister, Jacinda Ardern, who, aside from a quick and decisive effort against COVID-19, is the world's first elected head of state to go on maternity leave while in office.

She obliterates the notion that leaders cannot at once be tough, strong, and kind. *"Kindness, and not being afraid to be kind, or to focus on, or be really driven by empathy,"* she has said of what is at the heart of her leadership style. *"I think one of the sad things that I've seen in political leadership is – because we've placed over time so much emphasis on notions of assertiveness and strength – that we probably have assumed that it means you can't have those other qualities of kindness and empathy. And yet, when you think about all the big challenges that we face in the world, that's probably the quality we need the most."* [taken from "Seven Defining Characteristics of Jacinda Ardern's Leadership Style" (Susan Devaney, Vogue, 19 October, 2020: https://www.vogue.co.uk/news/article/jacinda-ardern-leadership-style)

Consistent with the theme of this book, it could be said that Ms. Ardern was guilty of Jaywalking in her approach to countering COVID. Rather than ignore, deny, or obfuscate, she was quick to get on top of the data that existed, and then talk very straightforwardly and decisively with her citizenry about what she knew, didn't know, and their first couple steps to counter the risk. Masks were involved, and she set the example. There was no striped crosswalk, no sign, no signal, she waded right out into a street named COVID.

What Ms. Ardern displays clearly is the fact that she is comfortable in her own skin, that she's willing to be a bit vulnerable, to say, "I don't know, but together we'll find out." As something of an aside, my experience with hundreds of CEO's suggests that leaders who can't get comfortable in their own skin by virtue of self-awareness tend to become petty tyrants with quite a trail of failed relationships and broken glass in their path.

> "The most important thing about leadership is your character and the values that guide your life. If you are guided by an internal compass that represents your character and values, you're going to be fine. Let your values guide your actions and don't ever lose your internal compass. Everything isn't black or white. There are a lot of gray areas in business."
>
> Brenda Barnes – former CEO, Sara Lee

Presence is Leading by Example

The meeting has barely begun, and you are already (conspicuously) glancing at your watch. If no one has ever told you, I will… that's a bad look. You leave the room to take a call that clearly could have waited. The report isn't quite the way you envisioned it, but you send it to the client anyway. Sound familiar?

With changing priorities, a breakneck work pace, and a relentless "to-do" list, leading by example isn't always the easiest thing for leaders to do. Yet in many cases, it's the foundation for respect and trust from others in the organization.

I know as well as anyone that it is a difficult example to set and keep, as there are near constant demands placed on your time, attention, emotions, your head and heartstrings, the list is endless.

How you handle that serves as an example, intended or otherwise, of what you'd like for them to do and be. Simply put, leaders who model desired behavior can more fairly expect the same in return. With integrity, conviction, and strength of character, leading by example is what transforms good companies into great companies. BTW, don't think for an instant that your people don't notice… they do, constantly, just like our children notice at home.

"People do what people see."

Joe Scarlett – Chmn. & CEO (retired), Tractor Supply Corp.

Live The Platinum Rule

While most of us remember the Golden Rule, I try (not always successfully), to keep faith with what has been termed the Platinum Rule - *"Do unto others not just as you would have them do unto you, but as they would want to be done to them."* It's a simple thought, yet one that resonates with everyone from parents raising children to employees looking to further a career. When leaders set the example of treating colleagues, superiors, and subordinates with respect, dignity, and kindness, others follow. Soon, it becomes the de facto standard.

Individual standards that serve as testaments to exceptional personal character translate into organizational norms and values. Honesty, generosity, and positivity are not mere words on a corporate plaque but part of the institutional fabric-reinforced from the top. If you're not actively (and consistently) demonstrating those qualities, you're better off taking the plaques down, rather than being guilty of insincerity, too.

As Leaders, We Have to Call It, In the Air

A store owner in *No Country for Old Men* (2007 neo-Western crime thriller film) unexpectedly encounters fate in the person of Anton Chigurh in the famous life or death coin toss scene. The owner is totally unprepared and tries to protest by saying *"I didn't put nothin' up."*

To which Chigurh replies, *"Yes, you did. You've been putting it up your whole life, you just didn't know it."*

In every life there are moments when fate throws us a curveball to which we must immediately respond. Decisions we cannot deliberate on, delay, or delegate. Often these moments require exceptional moral clarity and courage if a lifetime of painful consequence is to be avoided. Spiritual and career health, life, or death may hang in the balance.

We've been preparing for these moments our entire lives; many just don't know it. We fail to recognize that in all those "insignificant" choices between right and wrong, integrity or duplicity, we have been creating the character that will be revealed in our most trying moments of truth. That's the character that shows up, because it's all we've got.

Fate will visit us all with an unexpected coin toss and we will have to call it, in the air."

From *"The Power of Moral Leadership"* (R. Holley) Used with permission.

Reinforce Standards in Day-to-Day Operations

It's one thing to expect a certain level of performance from your team but it's quite another to model that behavior. Leaders who truly lead by example do so by reinforcing desired principles through their own words and actions. If you expect your team to stay in a meeting until it ends, do the same. If you expect the highest quality of work, then deliver no less yourself. When our teammates see organizational standards reinforced firsthand it resonates. Moreover, it suggests that you're serious, and not just mouthing platitudes, or a script. Leaders who consistently demonstrate things like integrity, conviction, decisiveness, and respect earn the benefit of the doubt.

Hands-On Leadership

As the top publisher of real estate advertising in the nation, and the largest printer in the State of Georgia, our firm, Network Communications, Inc. was open 24/7 365 days a year. Accordingly, as CEO, I felt it was important to visit operations at all different hours, not so much to check up on people, but to see firsthand how the various shifts worked, and as importantly, to let them know I cared about them, not as names on a payroll roster, but as real, pulsating human beings with faces, families, and lives outside of work.

I frequently went into the plant in the wee hours of the morning, on holidays, weekends, and any time I thought might gain the benefit of a real-world view of how the company and processes ran. Even more importantly, it was a tangible symbol of my respect for our team and their work. I wanted them to know that the guy who signed their paycheck cared enough about them and their work to come see for himself and be with them. That's one of the things that allowed Mr. McDonald to become Jay, and for the feedback that Jay got from the front line to be a whole lot more candid and spontaneous. Frankly, it kept our production leaders on their toes, too, knowing that their staff members knew me, called me by my first name, and felt free to initiate conversation, or even tell me things that I may not want to hear, but needed to know.

With 10 million magazines printed monthly and 35,000 photos processed each week, the team was often (I won't say always), okay, *sometimes* glad to have me there. I not only sat in, but after a while became proficient enough to help out with some real work with them, proofing, in the pre-press room, etc.

The point is that, by getting out of my office, I was able to see first-hand where disconnects were occurring, what worked well, and what needed help. Getting out there rolling up your sleeves and getting your hands dirty is an easy way to gain a comprehensive view of your organization from the inside, not to mention getting a little street cred. Whether it's a multi-million-dollar company or a small start-up, that time spent with the folks who are getting the real work done is time well spent for your knowledge base, employee relations, and for your clients.

> "Too often, people are assumed to be empty chess pieces to be moved around by grand viziers, which may explain why so many top managers immerse their calendar time in deal making, restructuring and the latest management fad. How many immerse themselves in the goal of creating an environment where the best, the brightest, the most creative are attracted, retained and, most importantly... unleashed?"
>
> – Gen. Colin Powell
> (US Army and US Secretary of State, retired)

(When was the last time you heard a military officer talking about unleashing talent? This man was truly special.)

Excellence is Seldom an Accident

High-performing organizations are the result of people at every level working as efficiently and effectively as possible. Trust is high, and individuals in every department want to work hard to meet objectives. As a leader, when your words and actions are inconsistent, trust erodes, friction creeps in, and employees begin to doubt the espoused organizational values that encourage things like hard work and high quality. Excellence is almost never an accident, but rather the result of leaders, at all levels, living the organizational values and doing what they say they'll do, every day.

> "We are often led to believe that sentiments like compassion and kindness are expressions of weakness rather than signs of strength. And we are often all too ready to give in to the false belief that meanness somehow equates to toughness and that empathy is empty of power..."
>
> Sen. Cory Booker - foreword, Compassionomics

The Power of Personal Presence

As noted earlier, positional power is giving way to the power born of presence, by which you are listened to, heard, and respected by teammates not so much for your job title or pay grade. Rather it is about who you are and your assured knowledge not just of yourself, but what you stand for, what you seek, ask, expect, and respect. Put simply, behaviors get results, not job titles.

This is an area, frankly, where by virtue of advanced emotional maturity (to include listening), in so many cases, women are contributing above their pay grade.

The Power of Optimism

An Asian proverb suggests that, "a man without a smiling face must not open a shop." I suspect the advice applies equally to female shopkeepers and know that it also applies to leadership. People simply will not follow a pessimist very far, or for very long. Why should they?

Think about it...There is a reason why parades tend to draw much larger and happier crowds than funerals. If you want people to follow you, it stands to reason that the better path is to give them something to invest their energy in and be joyful about, rather than depressed by. There's enough depressing stuff in the world. We needn't add to it.

WHAT?

1. Presence is about physically appearing on a regular basis, when it matters, and when/where you can do the most good. It's about how you handle your business.
2. Presence is a matter of caring, more doing, less telling.

SO WHAT?

1. Presence means bringing your best self, especially when it may be inconvenient or difficult to do so, or when you're scared, or you don't feel like it.
2. Be aware that you are on stage pretty much 24x7, with no do-overs for bad presence moments. Whether you did it, said it, or did not, people are watching.

NOW WHAT?

1. Find one or more devices that will serve as quiet reminders to you, unnoticeable to others, that you are on stage in your look, your manner, your words. I'm known to wear a rubber band on my wrist, or to put my watch on the opposite wrist as reminders to smile in tense situations.
2. If you need to work extra hard on this, ask a trusted confidant to help you by being especially observant and cueing you to aberrant or particularly successful behavior.
3. Use the whole matter of presence with your team to build esprit de corps, making it a point to show up as a sign that you care about them.
4. Be quick to coach leaders on the whole matter of presence, reinforcing the good, and correcting the bad. Don't wait for ill-advised, sub-optimum new behaviors to harden into habits. Similarly, be quick to recognize those that ought to be repeated.
5. Take pains to ensure that your calendar reflects personal presence as one of your top priorities. Show trumps tell.
6. Optimism attracts people who want to be in your company, on your team. Rather than merely "seeing the glass as half full), look for ways to expand the glass so it will hold even more, for more people. That's Jaywalking!

Chapter 12:
CLARITY
(This is a football)

The Bible's book of Proverbs, 29:18 suggests, *"Where there is no vision, the people perish."* Similarly, in the game of business, if not the larger game of life, where there is no well-shared and understood vision, where things like purpose, end goals, responsibilities, and outcomes are fuzzy, you typically lose the game, and probably the team as well. At the end of the day, our people want to read mysteries, not live them! We're no different.

"Our people want to read mysteries, not live them!"

-Richard Hadden, author - Contented Cows

The vision is where the leader or organization is headed, what's important, what you're striving for, and why. Why does it matter? What difference does it make? What difference does my effort, my part of this thing make? What's

---

the intersection between what I do and real, paying customers, and for that matter, end users?

I heard once of a consulting firm that was retained by a midwestern US plant of a major medical supply manufacturer to help discover the cause of and address product quality, productivity, and worker morale issues in the plant. After shadowing workers in the plant for a few days, observing normal operations, doing interviews with workers on the production line and their management, they were drawing blanks.

As they grew more desperate, a senior member of the team wondered aloud if anyone thought that the production workers saw a clear connection between their efforts to produce IV bag and tube assemblies, and the application of those devices with real, pulsating patients. Shrugs all around. "Let's find out," he said.

So, they rented a bus, a big, yellow school bus in fact, to take about 30 of the plant employees for a tour of a nearby county hospital. Within minutes of entering the hospital and seeing the intravenous bags and tubes that they had made providing life-giving nourishment and medication to sick patients, their heads began nodding with knowing validation of the importance of their work.

After similar tours for the remaining plant workers and some follow up meetings with their management to further explain the importance of their work, things made a decided turn for the better.

The lesson we can take from this is that people (all of us) need to see a clear connection between our work and real, paying customers, or end-users, or we're likely to conclude that what we do isn't all that important in the scheme of things, and the decline in our effort is at hand.

All of us need to see a clear connection between our work and real, paying customers, or we're likely to conclude that what we do isn't all that important in the scheme of things...

It's almost as if leaders with vision can see around corners. They see the larger game. They sense both possibilities, and risks. Hockey great and Jaywalker par excellence, Wayne Gretzky has been credited with saying that rather than waiting for the puck to come to him, he "skated to where the puck was going to be."

Great basketball players do the same, turning Jaywalking into an art form.

Jaywalking. Basketball 101 says don't make a pass to another player unless they are open and immediately available to receive the ball. (Stay within the lines.) The Jaywalked version says the player without the ball calls for it and immediately proceeds to the basket for an overhead pass high above the rim, and subsequent dunk. Does it always work? Of course not, but the success rate is reasonable, it messes with your opponent's heads, and fans love it, guaranteeing a noisy building for a while. The leader's purpose, as expressed to the players is to frustrate opponents defensively, score points against them, and create noisy fan support. Ding, ding, ding!

Strategic. Picture your playing field from ground level, then try to imagine it from an altitude of 35,000 feet, a common altitude for cross country flights. You can see lots more from up there, but you don't see it quite as well or with as great a degree of detail. So, your mind must fill in some of the blanks to achieve clarity. As you're filling in the gray spaces for the folks on your team, listen to former PepsiCo CEO Indra Nooyi, who underscores the importance of being candid: *"The one thing I've learned is don't lie to the people... Don't tell your people one thing when the reality is something different."*

Many people have a vision. The difference makers are those who can credibly articulate it and get others (not just a few, but everybody) to see it, believe it, and Commit (capital C intentional). Oftentimes, we're well-advised to color the picture in big, bold, colorful, read SIMPLE strokes.

On day one of training camp for his new team, the Green Bay Packers, who just months prior had lost in the final minutes of the league championship game, coach Vince Lombardi held up a football for the assembled team and announced, *"Gentlemen, this is a football"*, signaling a reset and a return to the most fundamental basics of the game.

In today's world where the airwaves are jam packed with messaging "content", leaders must find ways to reduce the noise, amplify the signal, and be taken seriously, quickly, and memorably.

One ultra-simple device I've used rather successfully is to regularly ask in the workspace a handful of employees to tell me their unit's three top priorities (just three), and then examine their answers for consistency from one to the other, and then with management's declared priorities (if any). The purpose is not so much to test them as to test the degree to which their leaders are communicating the right stuff and then making meaning with it.

This exercise gets really interesting when it's done in the boardroom with the senior leadership team. I ask each member to take out a sheet of paper and list the organization's three top priorities. When they've completed the task I gather the responses, lay them face down in front of the Chairman or President, and offer to bet him (sadly, it's still almost always a fella) a sizable amount of money that the responses are not all the same.

Having done this dozens of times, no exec has ever taken the bet! They didn't get there by being stupid, but it begs the question...when the top dozen or so people in the organization can't reliably articulate from memory the top three priorities, how can the thousands of people who report to them possibly know what they are and help accomplish them?

It's our job to find a way (make that ways) to articulate that stuff in clear and compelling fashion to the folks on our team. Don't wait for permission from on high or a fancy corporate program. Do it. Some of the best CEO's I've run into, by their own admission spend more than half their time doing this, and probably 50x the time consumed by deal making.

When the top dozen people in the organization can't reliably articulate from memory the top 3 priorities, how can the thousands of people who report to them possibly help them accomplish those things?

Show Beats Tell

"There seems to be no shortage of people out to change the world. Yet, just trying to change one other person typically produces an understandably defensive response. Imagine telling a group of people how screwed up they are, how enlightened I am, and expecting a positive response.

How about "show" rather than "tell?" That approach is what keeps people engaged, and why a leadership example is far more credible and compelling than the most eloquent verbiage.

Or rather than change the world, how about shine a light? *"Discover where our unique gifts best meet the needs of others and focus on making that light as clear and bright as possible. That's how MLK, Mother Teresa, and others who changed the world did it from the most unlikely places."* Roy Holley, *The Power of Moral Leadership.*

There's a bit of balance that needs to take place between being humble and knowing your own self-worth. Sure, you need to know your strengths and talents and when asked, you must tout those qualities! But there's a way to do it so that it is more effective and meaningful. So how do you maximize your strengths and showcase them in a modest yet effective way?

Personalize It

We had a speaker at one of our meetings who mentioned something brilliant that I had never thought about: She said that the brain processes information in very different ways, yet it tends to process visual things faster than any other medium.

That means if you can envision something, even if it's just in your head, chances are that you "get it" instantly. How is this relevant? By painting a picture using examples, you can personalize your story, thus making it easier for you to get your message across-and understood-quickly and efficiently. Better yet, tell your story in a way that directly connects you to your audience.

Paint A Picture Of Expertise

If you need to highlight expertise or a certain skill but don't want to portray yourself as "exceptional" or "highly skilled" try illustrating the concept instead. For example, if asked about customer service expertise you can share an example of how you saw a situation handled expertly, or how you experience customer service, and why it's important. By vividly using a shared, common real-life example, you can frame your message in a more understandable and useful manner.

One good method is to use questions or analogies. For example, if you worked in a retail store and wanted to emphasize your customer service skills you might ask "Have you ever been in a store looking for something and couldn't find anyone to help you?" Give an example of how you approached this with a customer and what you did to resolve the issue.

Painting a picture of expertise isn't bragging, but instead, sharing real-life information about something that you, or someone else accomplished. In the case of customer service, you get the point across that you care, but also that you're willing to go the extra mile to make sure that your customers are delighted. Chances are that customer will tell more people about the great experience.

The individual(s) to whom you are relating the story will be able to vividly see your commitment, creativity, passion, and the results. They will also appreciate your candor and humility in pointing out situations where you've had to learn a lesson the hard way. In fact, given the choice, I like to lead with one that didn't go so well, and leave them with one that did.

Another way to show people how, through their work, they are creating value for others is to let them share in the rewards. Over the course of my career, I have participated in dozens of schemes and programs whereby people are recognized via stock and cash grants, profit sharing checks, and spot cash awards for individual and collective meritorious performance. In the main, such programs rely on the basic tenet that, by and large, humans do what they are incentivized to do, all of us.

When people can easily connect the dots between their effort via their regular work, or through contribution of ideas that benefit the organization, and the reward itself, the clarity and priority of purpose is enhanced.

As President of C&S Bank, Mills Lane was in the habit of personally emptying out the suggestion box in the bank's offices, evaluating the suggestions therein, and then directly awarding employees with shares of the company's stock. Every time that happened, someone was both rewarded, and reminded what we were in business for.

And some are no doubt thinking how old-fashioned and downright boring this sounds. Funny thing, no one ever complained or refused the cash or stock.

I've done the same in my companies over the years, often providing workers significant profit-sharing distribution ahead of shareholders and management.

A friend's son who is in the restaurant business has been known to tape a certificate for a free pair of concert tickets to the back of a broom handle, lean it up against the wall, and the first person to pick the thing up and use it goes to the show. Clarity.

Though bureaucracy can be stifling, sometimes it's necessary, in small doses. Several years after ADP, the payroll and accounting services company he co-founded had gone public and was quite successful, Henry Taub was spotted one day walking through the company's Clifton, NJ headquarters. Every time he bumped into an employee who had been with him since the early days, he would reach in his pocket, pull out a $50 bill and reward the person on the spot for their service and longevity.

After this had been going on for a day or two, the company's Director of Employee Relations pulled the founder aside and explained that he couldn't just go around handing out cash to some, and not others, at which point the founder reminded the man of their respective positions on the org chart, and handed him a signed note directing the company's treasurer to equip this guy with as many $50 bills as he deemed necessary to similarly reward any employee who came to him and complained about having been left out. At last word, no one had ever done so. Some might call that Jaywalking.

WHAT?

1. Your people want to read mysteries, not live them.
2. For many of us, the brain seems to process visual information faster than other mediums. Show beats tell. That said, kinesthetic, and auditory modes must be included as well.

SO WHAT?

1. If your teammates can't explain the team's three (just 3) highest priorities, they can't possibly help accomplish them.
2. If they can't, the failure is likely on the part of leadership.

NOW WHAT?

1. Make sure that your people, all of them, can see clear linkage between their work, real, paying customers, and end users. Check regularly.
2. Take steps to become a better, more practiced, and visual storyteller.
3. Regularly ascertain whether your teammates can recall and explain the team's three highest priorities and relate their part in achieving them. If they can't, it's on you, not them. Own it, fix it, right away.
4. Try to picture your organization's work process from a 35,000' level and see where the process logjams and uncaptured opportunities are, then go to work on them. Become expert at explaining this in simple terms and visuals (try using crayons).
5. Be on a regular search for ever better ways to remind people of the organization's raison d'etre, goals, where they fit in, and why their work matters. Similarly, use a combination of programmatic incentives and spot awards to further clarify purpose and reward good work.
6. Be on a relentless search to identify and mitigate "noise" that impedes message flow.

Chapter 13:
DECISIVE
(Three, two, one, Go!)

*"Making no decision is in itself a decision,
and usually the wrong one."
— Frederick W. Smith - Founder & Chairman, FedEx*

Leaders get paid to think, and to use the outcome of that thought process to make timely decisions, to be decisive, to lead. Break a little glass. Pursue 70%+ solutions. If you can get to "perfect" in a reasonable time and manner, great, but in most cases, perfect is unattainable and 70% is a pretty good start.

Being wishy-washy or indecisive is not a good look for a leader at all. Indecision can burn up precious time that costs first mover advantage, or even just the ability to react to something. Moreover, it's not a good habit for Jaywalkers, and aggravates your teammates, as they realize all the while who's going to have to make up for the lost time and misdirected effort.

The vacuum that's created by indecision can suck the energy and confidence right out of a team. I've seen it happen up close. It takes forever to get that mojo back.

Decisions should be rooted in strong values, good information (data), and rational process. Weakness of character cannot be hidden. Leaders are often faced with tough choices and therefore must have the sound framework and the unfettered, unfiltered honesty from others to consider when making them. We must have the self-confidence tempered by humility to surround ourselves with those who will tell us the truth…and not sugarcoat it.

> "As a person who is sometimes in the room,
> I think one of the things that I do in the room
> is to talk about uncomfortable truths."
> – Darren Walker, CEO, The Ford Foundation

In an interview for Vistage members, former US military leader and Secretary of State, Colin Powell, one of the best leaders the world has ever known, encouraged use of the following decision model where the decision period is influenced by a probability of success range P=40 to 70, in which P stands for the probability of success, ranging from 40% to 70% based on the information then in hand.

According to General Powell, *"Once you have sufficient information to put the likelihood of success in the 40 to 70% range, go with your gut."* Further, he advised against acting *"if you have only enough information to give you less than a 40 percent chance of being right"* but, and this is critical, *"…don't wait until you have enough facts to be 100 percent sure, because by then it is almost always too late"*, and you will likely have sacrificed both safety and any first mover advantage.

It's analogous perhaps to an aircraft taking off. If a pilot were to attempt takeoff with a fully loaded Boeing 737-700 aircraft after a short takeoff roll of say, 800 feet, or 10% of an 8,000-foot runway, the aircraft simply would not rise from the ground due to insufficient speed, airflow and lift beneath the wings.

Conversely, if that pilot in the same aircraft were to use up every inch of runway gathering speed and then lift off, they would likely have wasted better than half the runway, and more importantly, any opportunity to immediately return to the ground in the event of an emergency or malfunction would be foreclosed, as would the ability to clear trees or tall structures in the runway path. Having been on the flight deck of an aircraft that has taken off long, and then experienced an engine fire as it was lifting off the ground, I can assure you, access to that runway can be important.

As it turns out, General Powell is not the only one with this point of view:

> *"When you can make a decision with analysis, you should do so. But it turns out in life that your most important decisions are always made with instinct, intuition, taste, heart."*
>
> Jeff Bezos

Abner King. CEO of Syringa Hospital and Clinics - Grangeville, ID (and not Jeff Bezos): *"The advice I wish I had been given before I started my role is: A good plan now is better than a great plan too late. As a rookie CEO of a small rural hospital, I often wanted all the questions answered, all the information at hand, before moving forward with implementing a major plan. The reality is that there will always be some degree of uncertainty, and some opportunities evaporate if you take too long to make your move."*

Andy Cochrane. Chief Hospital Officer of North Memorial Health - Robbinsdale, MN: *"One piece of advice is something that I think I knew as common sense but something I've learned the importance of multiple times in my career: The key to being your best as a leader is surrounding yourself with talented people and supporting them in being their best. Leading is all about inspiring and supporting, not just about making big decisions. It's advice I give any younger leader starting out."*

Exemplars

Consistent with a central premise of this book about the quick eating the slow, being quick requires being decisive, with a thoughtful, deliberate decision process, followed by data-driven reviews, probably with greater frequency and rigor than most of us are accustomed to.

Indeed, the global experience during the first year of the 2020 pandemic, indicated that where leaders reacted quickly and affirmatively to the virus and to their own populations, the resultant experience was generally far better than where leadership ignored, navel-gazed, or denied its very existence.

To be sure, the example of NBA commissioner Adam Silver on the evening of March 11, 2020, breaking the metaphorical glass and pulling the alarm lever to halt professional basketball in mid-air served as a clarion call to the world that the COVID19 virus was real, dangerous, and that it required immediate attention. Thankfully, much of the world took heed of his warning, New Zealand's young Prime Minister, Jacinda Ardern among them.

Ms. Ardern did a masterful job of announcing a bold set of initiatives intended not just to minimize the virus, but to eliminate it from the island nation of 5 million residents. Moreover, she exercised clear leadership by setting an example in donning a mask and imploring fellow countrymen to do the same. As a way of demonstrating her belief in the notion that in times like that, leaders should "bleed first and most" she imposed a pay cut on her own salary.

A majority of North American and European executives surveyed in December 2020 by McKinsey said their speed of making and implementing decisions was somewhat or significantly faster yr/yr, with an expectation that headline productivity will rise as a result. It did.

*Bloomberg: **US May See Post-Pandemic Productivity Surge, McKinsey Says** by Rich Miller, March 30, 2021

Speaking of Quickness and Resilience in their 4th "Annual Readiness Report", Deloitte posited that, *"Perhaps most importantly, the data suggests that speed matters. Organizations that made early investments in resilience related strategies during the COVID-19 crisis—or, even better, **had already made** strategic, workforce, and technology investments in capabilities that* enhance resilience—outperformed their competition. This finding points to a fundamental lesson that the pandemic brought home: That resilience is as much about thinking ahead as it is about doing what it takes to respond and recover from a crisis."

> "This pandemic has accelerated time, unmasked those who are in leadership positions, and revealed their authentic character."
>
> Harry Flaris

Standing Ovation

On August 14, 2021, as this book was in initial edit, a 7.2 level earthquake struck the island nation of Haiti, killing more than 1,200 people and doing massive structural damage on the island. Within two (2) days, crews from World Central Kitchen (@WCKitchen), an emergency food services cooperative organized by Chef Jose Andres after an even larger quake had struck Haiti in 2010, were on the island getting meals and vital supplies to Haitian residents.

An American business icon, born and raised in Mississippi, Jim Barksdale comes equipped with polite, folksy mannerisms that one might expect with his heritage, together with outstanding communications skill, and not infrequently, the most active braincells in the room. His career track includes important roles at IBM, FedEx (COO), McCaw Cellular (CEO), Netscape (President & CEO), the Barksdale Management Corp. (Chairman), and a variety of corporate and civic boards.

Mr. Barksdale has long demonstrated uncanny ability to inspire management teams to act decisively, and at times boldly, often using folksy metaphors as one of his levers of choice. He's known by those who've worked with, for, and around him for what have been termed, "Barksdaleisms."

One quite popular example includes the "3 Laws of the Snakes" which he has been known to apply to myriad business situations: (1) Don't go looking for snakes, but when you see a snake, do NOT call a staff meeting or play with the snake. Kill it, immediately! (PETA activists, please note, this is but a metaphor, and no snake disrespect is intended.) (2) Once they have been dispatched, do not play with dead snakes. No visitation, viewings, reincarnations, memorials, or anniversaries. (3) Always remember that many really good ideas start out life looking like... you guessed it, snakes.

He's renowned for using the second of the above "snake rules" as a lever to keep old, pet snakes from being revisited in the current decision process, speeding things up immensely.

I have it on good authority that fifteen minutes alone with Mr. Barksdale can be equivalent to a semester of B-school.

Before his death in 2016, business executive and former Columbia University football coach, Bill Campbell, who over the years coached several executives, among them Sundar Pichai, CEO of Google, maintained that one of the central tenets of leadership is the responsibility to "break ties" where the organization finds itself on the horns of a dilemma, and people are passionately and persuasively to'ing and fro'ing.

Pichai notes that the use of virtual meetings makes it considerably more difficult to get well-rounded input because it's easy within the context of the virtual space for the leader to overlook those who sit quietly 'in their box.' *"I've had to rethink a lot in the context of virtual meetings,"* Pichai says. *"Virtual meetings are harder, because everyone's looking at the person leading the meeting. And while some naturally participate, others hold back. I try to bring those people in, to make sure everyone participates."* "The Emotional Intelligence of Google CEO Sundar Pichai" by Justin Bariso, INC.

Though virtual meetings by necessity became outrageously popular in 2020, there is little doubt that they are here to stay, making Mr. Pichai's advice good for the short and long term. In fact, I did thirty minutes of coaching with an executive client recently on this very subject. There are a handful of counter-intuitive factors to deal with in this medium, not the least of which is the importance of maintaining near constant eye contact NOT, as usual with your audience which is pictured on the screen, but with the camera lens, which is the real 'front door' to your audience. And yes, know, for many of us, the lens is but a few short inches away from the screen on our laptop. It's still noticeable, trust me.

Decisiveness Matters

In 1982, four-year-old Jonathan Keane who, with his father, was attending a Boston Red Sox game was struck in the head by a hard, line drive foul ball off the bat of player, Dave Stapleton.

Red Sox Hall of Fame player, Jim Rice, who was on the field adjacent to Jonathan and his dad reached into the stands, lifted the child from his dad's arms and took him directly into the team's dugout where immediate medical attention was initiated. Though seriously injured, the boy managed a complete recovery after a hospital stay, thanks to the decisive action of Jim Rice and the Red Sox team doctor.

WHAT?

1. Making no decision is, in itself, a decision, and usually the wrong one.

2. In general, the closer decision making can be located at or near the "front door", the better.

3. We can seldom afford an unlimited fact gathering process in advance of our decision-making. Consider using a rule of thumb whereby we strive to gather enough data to put the odds of a successful decision into the 40 – 70% range, and then pulling the trigger with a nod to our gut instinct.

SO WHAT?

1. Though it's important to encourage front-line leaders to make decisions, senior leaders are frequently the ones who find it necessary to step into an internal debate, part the waters, make a decision, and get about the process of execution on that decision.

2. Organizations permeated by fear will tend to be quite a bit slower to make and execute decisions, usually requiring earlier senior level intervention in order to dissipate the perceived risk.

3. The better the people around you, the better (and quicker) your decision processes (and execution) will be.

NOW WHAT?

1. Look to the examples of Adam Silver (NBA), Jacinda Ardern (New Zealand PM), and Chef Jose Andres' World Central Kitchen (WCK) as exemplars for decisiveness in the face of COVID-19.

2. Rather than leaving a decision timeframe to the whims of an indeterminant fact gathering process, decide up front what data is to be gathered, how long that should take, and set a target date for the decision.

3. Be careful that "dead snakes" don't reincarnate and impair your decision processes.

4. Organizations are well-advised to vest front line workers with considerable decision authority for reacting to and resolving tactical customer and safety issues.

Chapter 14:
A COACH
(Here, play this!)

*"The two most powerful things in existence:
A kind word and a thoughtful gesture."*
– Ken Langone

Many of today's best leaders are completing a long overdue transition from straw boss (command and control) to being a coach who gives direction, encouragement, feedback, and facilitates learning by stretching (challenging) people in a positive, less formal way. Coaches provide candid feedback alongside different perspectives, experiences, and points of view. Most often, the coach is *not* furnishing a direct answer or solution as much as a path for the "player" to follow to reach a self-determined course. In other words, we're trying mightily to treat people as the adults we thought they were when we hired them.

In the same fashion that college (even middle school) athletes will switch schools to be with a better coach, our players in the workplace will, too, especially the better ones. They've got options and aren't afraid to use them. Indeed, a substantial amount of the job turnover that occurs today is not so much people leaving a job, but leaving their manager. Nobody wants to be around, let alone work with or for a "leader of last resort." Typically, those displaying higher aspirations expect a lot of coaching that is oriented to obtaining their next job. If they find that they aren't getting it, they make a move, and trade their manager in on a new one.

I don't want to make too much of it because at some level the analogy breaks down, but coaching people in the workspace is a not too distant relative of coaching athletes.

For too long, the focus of coaching was almost exclusively on dealing with problem behavior and performance. I'm not about to suggest that coaching weaker performers isn't important, because it is, but it misses a much wider area of opportunity to further develop talent, ALL of it, not just marginal performers or those who've hit a rough spot in the road. Besides, if all people hear is a nonstop litany of things they've screwed up, they quickly tune you out.

One concept that has understandably been getting a lot of attention lately is organizational trust. Especially in many of today's biggest companies, there is a trust deficit where employees, mid-level managers, even senior executives lack adequate confidence to do their jobs in all but the very best of circumstances. I know, I talk with them just about every day. That confidence deficit emanates largely from inadequate (fake it 'til you make it) preparation, in tandem with abject fear of making mistakes.

One of the imperatives of Jaywalking is that in order to take the training wheels off and cross the street without autopilot, our teammates (regardless of level) must trust their own ability, and those around them, their teammates/leaders to have their back. We must do no less for *everyone* in the organization.

As leaders, we must have confidence and trust in our people and we need to create an environment where innovation, creativity, and self-assurance attract the best and brightest. Businesses grow best when employees grow with it, yet not trusting is all too commonly a mistake made first by leadership. Strong leadership depends on a qualified team, their decisions, and their ability to get things done.

Beginning in mid-2020, millions of workers the world over were unexpectedly sent home, many with the expectation that, for the time being, that would become their new workplace, and it did. By and large they rose to the task… Stuff got done and business was handled, often at higher levels of productivity and quality than in more normal times. Hmm.

My hope is that, on the strength of that performance, which has been sustained for better than a year, managers can lose some of the implicit mistrust of our teammates, and the attendant mindset that has for so long caused us to adopt methods more apropos to supervising children than coaching and leading adults.

Coaches, Not "Supervisors"

The primary vehicle by which we can do that is by learning/adopting a coaching mindset and methods that will simultaneously enhance our ability to help teammates improve both their work performance and career potential.

Trust Is Essential to Growth

It's nice to know that the work you delegate, or the team you assign can get the job done. But there's more to trust than knowing a positive result will occur. Without trust and confidence, even the best leaders flounder as they can't keep the pace necessary to sustain a growing, thriving organization. There are only so many hours in each day, and leaders who lack confidence in their team try, and inevitably fail to do everything on their own. At that point, they become just another pair of hands.

Retain Great Talent

If you deny your people the freedom and flexibility to use some of their own judgment and to pursue their work confidently, the good ones will leave. Repeat, the good ones will leave, quickly. Without ample latitude and the ability to "break a little glass", employees will feel frustrated and unsatisfied. Those that do stay will never go above and beyond, resulting in a mediocre organization where "exceptionalism" has left the building.

Build Tomorrow's Leaders Today

A primary role of any leader is to develop future leaders and grow the organization forward with the best, brightest, and most engaged talent. If the mindset is to look inward and do everything alone, by definition, you limit your ability to hire, let alone retain great people, and build a team that can grow both the top and bottom lines.

The greatest, most successful leaders build high-performing organizations by trusting their team. Failure to effectively delegate both tasks *and* responsibility is a critical mistake made by too many leaders. Balancing delegation with risk, having qualified people to delegate to, and giving them the latitude they need to create, excel, and grow is fundamental.

Besides, one of the greatest things about leadership and trust is the fact that once you make a decision, you usually have the opportunity to make more. No organization can have long-term success without building a team of capable leaders. Growth both personally and organizationally comes primarily by developing leaders and employees whose efforts, talents, and results are expanded geometrically. In virtually all situations "we" is a far more powerful tool than "me!"

WHAT?

1. Owing to increasing complexity and pace of change, leadership is evolving from the role of straw boss to charismatic leader, to coach, in a less formal but much more responsive working partnership.

2. The latest iteration emerges from structural change in the employer/employee relationship from a paternalistic model to one that is less relational, more transactional, with shorter-term focus, resulting in constant restocking of the player roster and need to devote greater attention to short cycle skill development.

SO WHAT?

1. The "people quotient" for today's leaders is considerably greater today.

2. Due to a more "sensitive" workforce and a less skilled management cadre, many organizations have abandoned merit-based pay and the attendant regular work performance feedback, resulting in pay compression of high and low performing workers and considerable leakage of skilled, higher performing talent.

3. Leaders who are in the process of becoming coaches should work hard at the mechanics, especially timing, listening, asking good questions, and encouraging people to take some ownership of the discussion.

NOW WHAT?

1. Leaders at every level are encouraged to build their coaching skills via a coaching model that provides a predictable path to change.

2. Organizations are advised to have active, ongoing, developmentally oriented performance discussions AND resume merit-based pay schemes. If good performance isn't acknowledged, it won't continue.

3. Leaders should be prepared to recognize and deal with those who can't or won't succeed in a coaching environment.

4. Focus on the top performers.

Chapter 15:
RESILIENT
(Which way is up?)

"Resilience is very different than being numb. Resilience means you experience, you feel, you fail, you hurt. You fall, but you keep going."
– Yasmin Mogahed

Two words often get overlooked when we talk about the great innovators - Failure and iteration. Think about any great discovery, product, or service, dig into its history, and inevitably you'll find case after case of a cycle that features a launch followed by crash, burn, recovery, and reload. Whether it's Elon Musk of Tesla and SpaceX fame, Steve Jobs (Apple), Walt Disney, Fred Smith of FedEx, and Oprah (Harpo Productions), they all got knocked down or drew a bad hand, got up off the mat, shook it off, and got back in the game. If we're to lead our team very long or far, and be any sort of change agent, we must be prepared to do the same.

On his website, https://steveharvey.com/the-apollo-story-motivated/, entertainer, Steve Harvey tells a story of a period when he was down and out, had $35 to his name, no visible prospect to earn more, all of his worldly possessions would fit into two Hefty garbage bags, and yet, resultant from some persistence and hustle on his part, a series of phone calls and putting one foot in front of another led him to a full time gig at New York's Apollo Theater.

Not unlike Mr. Harvey, leaders are a bit like surfers. You paddle out, scout the waves, pick one, and get up on your board, without really knowing how it's going to end up. The ride is usually over when the wave says it's over. One thing we must be comfortable with is the reality of knowing that we very well might get knocked on our tail, and find ourselves upside down, beneath a few tons of cold, foaming seawater. And in those moments, we've got to find the ability and mental calm to protect ourselves, get reoriented, back on the board, look out for our team, and head back out. FYI, two of our first concerns are: Which way is up, and where did my bathing suit go?

"New Coke"… If It Ain't Broke

In 1982, the Coca-Cola Company, another fine, Atlanta-based organization introduced Diet Coke, which for nearly 40 years has been an immensely popular (and profitable) beverage line extension.

Following on three years later, the company introduced a reformatted beverage that was intended to take the place of the original Coca-Cola which had been delivered the same way for 99 years. Almost immediately it became apparent that, somehow, despite spending millions of dollars on product research, focus groups, and pre-launch advertising, the company had absolutely, positively fumbled the ball, er bottle.

Beyond being disappointed, Coke customers were furious, and more than a little vocal about how much they disliked the change and wanted "the real thing" back. In retrospect, in some parts of the world Coke might have had an easier time had they said, "We're going to take your *water* away."

Seventy-nine days later, the company deftly reintroduced the original beverage as "Coke Classic" thus dousing the flames of customer ire. Then Chairman and CEO, Roberto Goizueta remarked, *"We set out to change the dynamics of sugar colas in the United States, and we did exactly that — albeit not in the way we had planned."*

Burn Down the Mission

Continuing, he added, *"But the most significant result of 'new Coke' by far was that it sent an incredibly powerful signal ... a signal that we really were ready to do whatever was necessary to build value for the owners of our business."* https://www.coca-colacompany.com/company/history/the-story-of-one-of-the-most-memorable-marketing-blunders-ever

Because Coca-Cola was smart about keeping its options open, it was able to quickly shift course and reintroduce Coke "Original", thus holding on to their loyal consumer base, and becoming stronger in the process.

There have been similar missteps of this magnitude by other Fortune 500-sized companies in that same era (e.g., FedEx's failure of its ubiquitous fax service, "ZapMail") which led to some very red faces in Memphis, in addition to hundreds of millions in red ink. In each case, by staying clear-headed, nimble, and responsive, the managements involved were able to narrowly avoid disaster and continue apace, wiser for the experience.

Despite deep expertise, leaders in every industry and occupation will make mistakes. We've had spaceships blow up on launch, aircraft manufacturing flaws that caused fatal accidents, and viruses that were allowed to get totally out of control. Organizational leaders are expected and paid to take (and manage) these risks.

One key to bouncing back after a blunder is to thoroughly evaluate and quantify risk. We must quickly be candid about misfires, while understanding that there are always multiple stages on the path towards a decision for modifying, tweaking, and innovating for a better outcome. Talking about the New Coke affair after the fact, Mr. Goizueta allowed that, *"Sometimes you must be willing to risk looking foolish to become knowledgeable."* Such is the price of education.

> *"Sometimes you must be willing to risk looking foolish to become knowledgeable."*
>
> Roberto Goizueta

GE and Jeff Immelt: Fear is Debilitating

With his tenure in the corner office starting just four days before 9/11, Jeff Immelt was CEO of GE from 2001 to 2017, replacing the highly touted and revered, but feared Jack Welch. Relative to getting dealt an early tough hand with 9/11, Immelt suggested that when in rough water, a leader *"has to absorb fear"* because fear is debilitating, and will cause a team to freeze usually at precisely the wrong time. I don't agree with Mr. Immelt on a lot of things, but he's so right on this point.

During his seventeen-year tenure at the helm, Immelt accomplished a lot principally simplifying GE's business footprint, extricating the company from several businesses which no longer (or perhaps never did) fit, including ultimately, GE Capital which went from lemonade to lemon in a big way. By his recollection, the company generated about $280 billion in cash on his watch, but ultimately, with the stock having lost about 2/3 of its value over the course of his tenure, the board ultimately and understandably asked him to step aside.

Mr. Immelt subsequently took some time to regroup, to think, and write while repositioning himself into a smaller, more malleable organization. His book, *"Hot Seat: What I Learned Leading a Great American Company,"* offers remarkably candid insight into some of the lessons he learned the hard way.

Dr. Ángel Cabrera and Mission-Inspired Resilience

In a June 2021 interview, Dr. Ángel Cabrera spoke at length with me about his approach to leadership and how that played out as the Pandemic came ashore in the US just months after he had assumed the helm as President of Georgia Institute of Technology. He told me, *"I'm a strong believer that one of the most important things the leader gets to do (or has to do right) is to get the mission and the vision right and to push that day and night, to have a strong sense of why we exist, and what it is we believe in."*

Barely six months into the process of ferreting that out, Dr. Cabrera's leadership was put to the test in seeing to the safety and continued productivity of 36,000 students (half of them online,) and 14,000 employees on three main campuses across the globe.

While the strategic thought process was derailed for a very short time as he put the Institute on *"war footing"* to address the conditions of the virus, Dr. Cabrera fortuitously saw that interspersing continued deep thinking about their mission, vision, and values was at once both highly useful to helping focus the school's energy, and therapeutic for the involved team members. In the process, their mission (see below) became the guiding beacon for their R&D efforts to develop important new medical capability that was almost immediately put to use combating the virus.

One of my own key take-aways from that conversation with Dr. Cabrera was a reminder that having a keen sense of mission is not only highly productive, but it can also have considerable calming effect amidst a storm. That's advice well worth remembering.

Georgia Tech's mission is, *"to develop leaders who advance technology and improve the human condition, with focus on making a positive impact in the lives of people everywhere."* https://www.gatech.edu/about

Dr. Ángel Cabrera's Results

How did his plan work? In his words in January 2021, "As the year unfolded, science helped us understand and combat the deadly virus. Thanks to biotechnology, we were able to roll out everything from massive testing and new treatments to data models and a novel vaccine that was developed in record time using a method never before employed (mRNA). Meanwhile, information technology kept us connected and productive. Many of us could keep working and learning, and we could shop, play, and be entertained as we stayed safely away from each other to avoid infection."

He continues, "As I try to digest and process the past few months, I keep coming back to the same idea: that it is the responsibility of leading institutions like Georgia Tech to advance science and technology, to find solutions to the most consequential issues of our time, to understand and mitigate the risks posed by those solutions, to inform the public, and to educate leaders who can make technology deliver on its promise. And this is precisely the core idea of our new strategic plan."

Resilience At a Young Age

Perhaps the best example of resilience that I'm familiar with presents in the form of Darren Walker, now CEO of the Ford Foundation, who was interviewed by Leslie Stahl of *60 Minutes* for a show that aired in April 2021. Here's an absolutely riveting section of the interview dealing with Mr. Walker as a young boy "meeting" his father for the first, and only time:

> "I met my father once. I was about four years old. And my cousin brought me by and said, "Joe, this is your son, Darren. And don't you wanna say hello to him?" And he wouldn't come out of the house. I actually never saw his face because the screen door covered most of his face."
>
> Darren Walker, CEO -The Ford Foundation

Take a moment to slowly re-read that last paragraph.

Lesley Stahl: *"That is so painful."*

Darren Walker: *"I think it's painful, but I think it's also-- there's a resilience that comes from that."*

Beulah Spencer (Darren's Mother): *"I knew the Lord had something good in store for Darren."*

The resilience really came, Walker says, from his Mother, Beulah Spencer

Beulah Spencer: *"Education, education, education."*

When dealing with adversity, we're well advised to:

1. Accept the situation for what it is, but not one drop more. Let's not add to our problems by becoming imprisoned within our own minds. US Navy pilot Capt. Charles Plumb, talks about his imprisonment in a Vietnamese prison camp and some dark periods when he had temporarily allowed his mind to fence him in even more than his captors had, by spending countless hours being angry at McDonnell Douglas for not building a sturdier plane, and the US Congress and President who had sent him overseas to prosecute a stupid war. To hear him tell it, he had built his wall of self-pity, brick by brick, nearly to the point that it could have consumed him. Capt. Plumb's ultimate survival relied upon a principle long espoused by Eleanor Roosevelt, "No one can make you feel inferior without your consent."

2. Don't lose your sense of humor. Capt. Plumb talks about the goofy games and mental diversions he and fellow captives resorted to just to get through the day during their imprisonment. In one such instance, they held a contest to ascertain which prisoner (again, they were mostly jet pilots) had punched out of their ride the highest and fastest, and who was the lowest and slowest. As he recalls, highest and fastest went to an Air Force jet jockey who exited at something like 11,000' and 0.3 mach, and lowest and slowest went to Seaman Douglas Hegdall who fell 26 feet from the fantail of his ship which was traveling at a speed of about 15 knots.

3. Be an optimist, and mindful of other tough scrapes you've encountered and survived. By all means, be realistic, but pessimism isn't your friend. To the contrary, it saps energy and gets in your way. One good way to combat this is to be a friend to someone else who is struggling even more.

4. Quickly take stock of your assets, your knowledge, and the information you do have, even if it's no more than knowing which way is up. When you're underwater, that's worth a lot. ☺

5. Don't be too proud to ask for help. We have friends for lots of reasons. This is one of them. I'm talking about the short list of real friends, not the Facebook variety; people you can phone at 3AM for any reason (or no reason), and they'll be there in an instant.

6. Refuse to give up. I've a friend whose 41-year-old daughter is a military wife, Mother to 5, and afflicted with end stage renal disease with no hope of a transplant. She was told years ago by knowledgeable docs to get her affairs in order. This woman gets up every morning after a couple hours of fitful sleep (at best), and goes into battle as a wife, Mom, and a homeschool teacher, who can't spell the word, "quit"! We shouldn't either.

WHAT?

1. A learned trait, resilience is the ability to pivot again and again to stuff happening. We can add a tail wind effect to our resilience by adopting a positive mental attitude or, a headwind by assuming victim status.

2. As Georgia Tech President, Dr. Cabrera pointed out, our ability to survive (even thrive) in difficult situations can be aided immensely by having an acute knowledge of our mission, values, and priorities.

SO WHAT?

1. As illustrated with the examples of "New Coke" and FedEx's ZapMail service, resilient organizations can take more swings via Strategic Jaywalking, knowing that they've got the ability to take a few steps outside the line or against the signal, and still recover if need be.

NOW WHAT?

1. Accept tough situations for what they are, but not one drop more. The 2020 -21 COVID Pandemic presented both risk and opportunity, the latter of which only became available to those who were willing to see the glass being half-full, or, better yet, see the possibility of a bigger glass.

2. Be like Darren Walker and the military wife/Mom with kidney disease. Don't even think about giving up.

3. Periodically exercise your resilience muscles to keep them in operating form. You never know when you're going to need them.

Chapter 16:
COMMUNICATOR
(You said what?)

A leader is nothing if not a communicator. Through a plethora of modes and platforms we gather, record, analyze, parse, and distribute information of all types - numbers, text, plans, feelings, visuals, you name it. We gather information for and from, and distribute information to our team, our peers, reporting seniors, as well as people outside the organization.

Regardless of form, it must be credible, complete, compelling, on time, and on point. Speeches, Zooms, emails, texts, reports, meetings, one to ones, all of it. With all kinds of people, not all of whom speak our language, dialect, or use the same devices. And not to strike undue fear in anyone, but one of the important lessons leaders must learn early is that you are no longer speaking just for yourself, but for the broader organization. It's vital that your perspective (and your courage) line up with that, even when you're not entirely sold on the message.

Our job in all of that is to make meaning. Simplify the complicated. Leaders (the good ones) don't just yap. More wordage is not necessarily better. They cut through the crap. They. Make. Meaning. They're good storytellers. They inspire and must be adept at doing so via whatever channel, platform, or device best suits each audience member at that particular moment.

> *"Never underestimate the power of a single light piercing the darkness."*
>
> Roy Holley - "The Power of Moral Leadership"

Let's give that another go for the sake of clarity. When it comes to making meaning, your preferred channel or style matters much less than the preferred mode or device of your *audience*. Otherwise, you could be guilty of speaking Greek via high tech device when you're in Texas during a power outage.

With so much of the world today, our choice of communication style and mode should be keyed to whatever device our audience members happen to have in hand at the moment. In so many respects, we're not only expected in a lot of cases to be multi-lingual, but to have multi-mode proficiency as well. To the multi-lingual item, if you do business in the US and aren't yet fluent in Spanish, get with it, and Mandarin isn't far behind.

That goes for video and videoconferencing as well. We no longer have the choice to do single-mode comms. In that vein, do not, repeat, do NOT be lulled into believing that, as sexy as it is, videoconference presos are an easy or simple affair. They require even more time and effort in preparation. Trust me on this. I've done some really good ones, and some complete clunkers. The difference is planning and preparation. You've gotta do the work. Effort matters.

As a benchmark, I routinely spend 100 minutes of preparation for every minute of a speech, more than that for video presentation. There's just more complexity, and things that can go wrong. That includes some heavy-duty rehearsal intended not to get to the point where I can get it right, but to the point where I can't get it wrong! And I'm not talking about simple memorization that leads to puking out a canned script.

Concise + Candor

Beginning in my time at Darden and continuing forward, I've found it beneficial to be direct, concise, and to speak truth with candor. (I'm still working on the concise part.) As leaders, we should give credit and take blame.

We should avoid "yes" people like the plague. Peter Drucker once said, "If you've got a yes person working for you, one of you is not needed."

It's important to share or even at times "overshare" information with your teammates. To be a great communicator, we need to get away from our comfort zone and mix with the folks who are making results happen, and those who may share a different view. How else are we going to really understand and appreciate their information needs? In the same vein, we must never become isolated from candid feedback.

Poor communication causes people to "fill in the blanks" with their own preconceived notions, perspectives, and fears. In nearly all cases, their filled in blanks will not mesh well with your reality. Don't keep things secret. Provide clarity of ideas and direction. Always try to simplify the complicated.

Speech as Artistry

Speaking about the 1996 Atlanta Olympic Games, an ultimate long shot that succeeded beyond anyone's expectations, organizer Billy Payne said, *"The real legacy of the Games is that the people of Atlanta felt for themselves the legacy of possibility."* **The legacy of possibility.** Our role as leaders involves painting just such a vivid picture of possibility for the folks on our team and in our audience.

All that said, as important as the emoting part is, good leaders are even better at listening *really* **listening**. And while we're at it, please listen to this:

In several decades of leading organizations and coaching leaders, I have seen more management careers derailed by the failure to listen than any other single cause.

Great Listeners

2 ears, 1 mouth. Listen to learn, not to respond (especially if you are married, or want to be.)

When you spend the bulk of your adult life in Atlanta, you're never far from the skilled professionals (and I dare say nice people) of Delta Air Lines, certainly to include Delta pilots, several thousand of whom call the ATL home. One thing that cannot escape you when interacting with pilots is their skill level in areas that may seem to have nothing whatever to do with flying an airplane, communicating for example.

When you give more than about two nanoseconds of thought to it, you realize that commercial aviation especially is a team sport, heavily dependent on comms that are both timely and precise. If, for example, at altitude, you see a band of unavoidable heavy weather about five minutes out, the cabin crew in the back would probably appreciate a heads up so they can get passengers and the aircraft cabin squared away without frightening anyone.

Similarly, when Air Traffic Control issues flight and clearance directives, as they do throughout the flight, it's vitally important for the flight crew to get it the first time, and it needs to be right, or bad things can happen. (Think ATC instructions slightly garbled by background noise arriving with a clipped, thick New York accent over the cockpit speakers (which aren't all that good) at the same pace at which you're able to read it here:

"Delta 955, turn left to two, seven, zero; Descend and maintain flight level two six zero, Contact Albuquerque approach at one, two, four point four." Click.

Did you get all that on one take? Would you bet a couple hundred lives, including yours on it? These guys and gals are really good.

Two of the best listeners I've ever known were executives who previously had been pilots, one a commercial passenger jet pilot (Arthur), and the other a US Navy and private jet pilot (Sydney). Each had their own habits for listening and registering the content of what they heard.

Something of a kinesthetic learner, Arthur preferred old school methods. He carried a deck of 3"x5" cards that served as a business card on one side, with blank space for notes on the other. It likely emanated from his experience as a pilot when he had similar cards clipped to a pilot's kneeboard strapped to his leg, for use when he got a string of instructions like the ones above.

Whenever you talked with him and mentioned something he thought was important or needed follow-up, one of those cards came out of his shirt pocket and, in a flash he was making a note. As importantly, he had a virtually foolproof system for following up commitments recorded on the cards, yours, and his both.

When in conversation with him and you saw one of those cards come out, you could be darned sure he was listening to every word, which actually feels pretty good. His writing the stuff down was in effect validating what you just said. And, not to put too fine a point on it, but when you committed something to him and it, too, took up residence on one of those little cards, you could be very sure that he, or someone on his behalf would soon follow up to check the status of your commitment, make that Commitment with a capital 'C'.

Sydney on the other hand was a master of face-to-face communications. First, his desk consisted of a 50" round oak table which presented a less imposing barrier between he and whomever he was meeting with. Silently, almost effortlessly, if his assistant hadn't already done so, he would remove everything but a fresh pad of note paper from the table before you sat down, thereby removing any possible distraction, and keep prying eyes away from whatever he was working on.

Sydney had mastered the process of asking really good, pertinent questions, then shutting up and listening, *really* listening (to understand, rather than respond.) On those occasions when he thought he had heard something that might be revelatory, with an almost patented move, he slowly removed his glasses, leaned in, looked you square in the eye, and with an innocent, inquisitive tone said, "Now tell me again, what did you just say?" At that point, like Arthur, the pad went to work.

Listening Tips:

- When listening to someone, look at them and notice their eye color. Somehow it aids listening, and sorry, I don't know why, but it does. Trust me and try it.

- Don't interrupt. Repeat, do not interrupt.

- Listen to understand, NOT respond.

- Listen for what was NOT said.

- When the other person stops talking, wait a moment (a 3-second count) before opening your mouth. Really, it won't hurt you. They won't be offended. Let her finish!!

- Ask questions to clarify what you think you just heard, or, put differently, simply say, "Tell me more about that."

That last little sentence alone can work wonders in your communication with teammates, together with your relationship with them. Put yourself in their shoes for a moment. What does it suggest when someone who is senior to you asks you to tell them more? It suggests to me that, A. They are listening, and B. They actually care what you have to say. Ding!

"Never be afraid of the conversations you're having. Be afraid of the conversations you're not having."

—Susan Scott, Fierce Conversations

WHAT?

1. All leaders have heavy communications obligations today. Part of that obligation involves cutting through the clutter, the noise, so as to be heard, and to allow others to be heard and understood.
2. Communication is more, much more than emoting. It's about making meaning, which also requires heavy doses of listening.

SO WHAT?

1. Two ears, one mouth: Used in that proportion, maybe even at a 6:1 ratio.
2. Preparation is key. Practice not until you get it right, but until you can't get it wrong!
3. More leaders fail due to poor listening skills and habits than anything else.

NOW WHAT?

1. When listening to someone, do NOT interrupt. Listen to learn, not to respond. Guys, this especially means you. Let her finish!
2. Use questions to clarify, or use the statement, "Tell me more."
3. Don't be afraid of the conversations you are having, but the ones you're NOT having.
4. Use whatever mnemonic device you find helpful to memorialize your discussion learnings. Then, get comfortable using it, as an everyday habit.
5. Communication is a skill that is enhanced with practice. You simply must put in the time and effort. Read, watch/listen to others more skilled than you, and "go to school" on them. If you want to accelerate the change process, work with a coach, especially for speeches and other presentations.
6. To learn more, I often say, "I don't know. What do you think?

Chapter 17:
MASTER OF TIME & PRIORITIES
(You want it when?)

"Make each day a masterpiece."
– John Wooden

Leaders learn that saying "no" is a big part of the job. It's not out of meanness, selfishness, or negativity, but conservation of time and energy relative to their priorities. If they fail to achieve and maintain a firm grasp of their priorities, the day soon comes when nothing is a priority and they are simply spinning their wheels, taking up space, going home tired, and at risk of getting voted off the island. Always remember... "NO" is a complete sentence.

But for a persistent failure to listen effectively, I've seen more leaders crash and burn due to an inability to maintain discipline in focusing on their priorities than any other cause. Quite often this happens when we neglect our priorities while in hot pursuit of today's "urgencies", which is a bit like giving up eating green beans for a bag of Cheetos.

You're asked and expected to attend meetings where you will play no part at all, other than to occupy a chair or merely give assent to something that could more easily be done by non-meeting means. Or worse, you organize the meetings where others are expected to do the same. Just don't.

Too often those things happen because we are social beings and find safety in numbers, or, because we've always done it this way. The XYZ meeting has taken place at 3 PM on Mondays forever. It's an institution. Face it, if two people put their heads together and make a dumb decision, at least one of them has a problem. If a group of two dozen folks get together, form a committee, and do the same dumb thing, they are able to create enough dust to disguise the dumbness.

> *"Never get so busy making a living that you forget to make a life."*
>
> *– Dolly Parton*

Here Are Three Simple Tips I Would Offer:

1. Maintain at all times a firm understanding and grasp of your top three (3) priorities, both in business and your personal life. If you can't name them readily off the top of your head and explain them with something as simple as a crayon, then they aren't priorities, and you aren't very serious about them.

2. Share those priorities, as appropriate, with those around you in both your personal and professional realms. In the case of the business realm, take pains to ensure that your reporting senior, board (whomever you answer to) is aware and in concert with those items. Check regularly for confirmation. This is one of the habits that makes Jaywalking considerably safer. Otherwise, if someone above you in the food chain has called an audible that you are unaware of, you can easily get caught in the middle of the street in rush hour dodging cars.

3. Take pains to see to it that your actions are largely in accordance with your priorities. Find a simple way that works for you to assess progress and missteps on this daily. (Yes, daily.) If you have the good fortune to have an administrative assistant, enlist their help in this regard.

"Your legacy is every life that you've touched. We like to think that these great, philanthropic moments are the ones that leave the impact, or will make the huge difference in the world, but it's really what you do every day. It's how you use your life to be a light to somebody else's."

Oprah

WHAT?

1. Next to poor listening, the inability to effectively manage one's time and priorities is THE top failure of business leaders.
2. From the moment you accept a leadership position, your time will be your most precious commodity. You'll become much more familiar with saying the word, "No." It is, after all, a complete sentence.

SO WHAT?

1. Neglecting priorities in favor of the day's "urgencies" is like passing up green beans for a bag of Cheetos. You'll be fulfilled for about 30 seconds.
2. It's vital to maintain a high correlation between daily activities and stated priorities, and not be magnetically attracted to our favorite things.

NOW WHAT?

1. If you have the good fortune to have the services of an executive assistant, involve them heavily in the management of your activities.
2. Take pains to share your plans and priorities both with your team and reporting senior.
3. Be certain to always know your top 3 priorities. It helps to be equally familiar with your boss's priorities, as they will tend to shape yours as well.
4. Treat other people's time with as much respect as you do your own. This will gain you immense appreciation and respect.
5. Build regular time into your schedule for thinking, yes, thinking.
6. On a regular basis, have the good sense to turn off the device!
7. At times you're asked to take on a significant task or project that you doubt you can give good attention to because of other committed priorities. Rather than quietly accepting the risk that you'll stumble, make them aware that completion of this new task will require you to re-prioritize other assigned objectives. If you need relief that would benefit you in accomplishing these things, this would be an excellent time to request it. Whatever you do, do not simply accept the new task without making your concern known, and then fail at it. That's a double whammy as you get dinged for failing, and dinged again for not telling anyone that you knew from the start that you lacked the resource or the runway to get it done.

Chapter 18:
ADEPT AT USING POWER
(I'll give you a reason)

"Leadership is the wise use of power. Power is the capacity to translate intention into reality and sustain it."
– Warren Bennis

Every leadership job worth having is vested with a certain amount of power and authority, the ability to make decisions on behalf of the organization in the interest of getting things done. Deciding priorities, assigning responsibility to teammates, acquiring assets, hiring teammates, deselecting teammates.

Your job contains "position power" that comes with the job description and paycheck, and "personal power" that is more commonly generated via relationships, respect, and guile, usually when you've earned the benefit of the doubt.

In and of itself, power is neither good nor bad. It's but a tool that can be used well and wisely, or with wanton neglect. I look at using power as analogous to using the accelerator pedal on an automobile. With a good sense of the vehicle's capabilities, the applicable policies/rules, and the road conditions, good leaders will use enough power to get the job efficiently, yet safely done.

The inappropriate use of power is a major derailer of leadership careers. A one end of the continuum are those who, perhaps fearful of making a mistake, can never seem to apply enough power to get the thing off the ground and up to speed. Their stylistic opposites seem destined to always show the world how much power they've got by using way more of it than necessary to get a job done. (Just look how powerful and important I am.)

Strange as it may seem, more leaders find their way into trouble not by using too much power, but by failing to use that which has already been entrusted to them. I see it with purchasing decisions for example, where some, despite having clear purchasing and budgetary authority granted them to do something, act out their insecurities or indecision by dawdling and playing "Mother may I?" Over time, that has the corrosive effect of actually diminishing their power and their stature, not to mention their ability to get things done efficiently.

Moreover, knowledge and information are as much levers of power as purchasing or hiring/firing authority. Leaders who are not adept at, or who practice 'old school' management by failing to distribute that power are effectively putting a crossing light with a constant red (check with me) signal at every intersection their people must use. This perhaps is the single most unwise use of power in the current workspace, and it is all too prevalent. Aside from slowing everything down, your better people will leave rather than spending half their day waiting for permission. Please don't do that. (End of rant.)

Alternatively, I would suggest that virtually everyone on the payroll should be vested with a reasonable level of authority to act on behalf of a customer... to spot a problem or potential problem, for example, and take direct and immediate action to resolve it. Will they always get it right? Of course not, but you wouldn't either.

Those prone to using too much power or using it inappropriately tend to be easier to spot, because not unlike with an automobile, when too much power is applied, there is often a lot of associated noise, and maybe damage.

Unlike a credit line at a bank, where using the entire line is generally frowned upon, leaders ought not be reticent to use (when necessary) the full measure of their leverage. I've found it helpful when doing so to at least alert my reporting senior or board of my intentions as a simple courtesy. In a similar vein, if I'm expecting to perhaps break an internal 'speed limit' or do something that might create a few waves, (serious or protracted Jaywalking) I'll usually pre-announce or pre-clear it with my leader just so they're not surprised. I'm not asking their permission per se, rather, giving them the courtesy of knowing what I'm about to do (and why), and yes, the opportunity to countermand it if they are so inclined.

Early on in a new business reporting relationship, you'll want to have some discussion with your reporting senior and those who report to you about the normative standards of authority. In one such conversation, I discovered that I was crosswise with a guy a couple levels above me who maintained somewhat militaristically that unless a company policy specifically permitted a certain action, it was forbidden. My view was diametrically opposed, such that unless an action was forbidden by policy it was inherently permissible. Suffice it to say that relationship didn't last long.

In another case, (pre-cell phone era) when serving as board chair of a private organization, I was faced with a need to make a rather significant capital improvements decision (board approved) AND a fortuitous opportunity to simultaneously make some additional necessary property improvements with a first-rate developer. The latter part was not yet board approved. Given a very short window of opportunity, I unilaterally approved the secondary part of the project, which raised the hackles of a few board members until such time as they saw the business case behind the decision, which was solid. In hindsight, I should have prearranged clearer lines of authority, and discretionary boundaries with my board. Sometimes we all learn by breaking a little bit of glass and having the opportunity to clean it up.

An aspect of power that I don't see being used effectively at all is "borrowing" the power of others by asking people above me in the food chain to sign on in support of something. Sometimes doing so can result in a win-win-win.

An example of such is when I want to call attention to something that someone on the team has done particularly well and deserves credit for. Rather than me offering the congratulations, I've been known to go over my head organizationally, and ask someone senior to me to provide the shout out. It gives the big shot an opportunity to get credit for doing something nice, it costs nothing, and it just knocks the socks off the individual being complimented. I've only been refused once when asking for this. (It was the same guy I described a few paragraphs above. ☺

One More Time

Power takes on a negative connotation when it is used for nefarious purposes, as in cases where organizational power is used for corrosive intent or purely personal benefit. Almost irrespective of the magnitude, such occurrences tend to have substantial downside consequences because the individual is branded by the act. Don't go there.

This advice is particularly apropos to personal behavior that has no business in the workspace. In August 2021 the world was witness to the Governor of New York, one of the most powerful people in the country, being driven from office by a multitude of sexual harassment complaints filed with the state's Attorney General by women who worked in his vicinity and chain of command. While there are a lot of mistakes that people will seek to understand and possibly forgive, that isn't one of them.

WHAT?

1. Be mindful and respectful of both your position power and your personal power. Treat them as business tools, which is exactly the way they are intended. Use them, but don't abuse them.

2. Be mindful of the extent to which power is well-shared throughout the organization, certainly to include with front line, customer facing employees, who should be able to spot and remedy workplace safety and tactical customer problems instantly. Will they always get it right? No, but you wouldn't either. Disbursing this power is a perfect example of Jaywalking. People shouldn't have to ask permission to do the right thing for a customer.

SO WHAT?

1. Power is entrusted to you not as a perk, but a tool that you are expected to use, but not abuse or for personal gain.

2. Wise leaders realize that over time they can actually grow their personal power by using it appropriately to do good things and generously including others in the credit.

3. Conversely, be careful not to abuse the power granted to you, or to use it inappropriately (e.g., for personal purposes, or anything that appears so.)

NOW WHAT?

1. Be on the lookout for situations where you can possibly get a win-win-win by making someone senior to you aware of an as yet unrecognized success in the organization, and asking them to join you in recognizing the responsible party.

2. Make it a point to ascertain early on the normative standards for using power in both individual and organizational relationships. Sometimes things aren't as they seem. Budgets can be a particularly thorny issue in this regard.

3. Periodically, take a step back and give thought to how power is distributed and used within your organization. Is it dispersed enough so that it can be applied within an everyday context, or are business processes being unnecessarily slowed by people waiting on a crosswalk signal (decision) that should be made a little closer to the action?

4. Given sufficient justification to do so, don't be bashful about asking for additional authority to accomplish assigned objectives.

Chapter 19:
CONFIDENT
(But of course!)

"Do one thing every day that scares you."
– Eleanor Roosevelt

Mrs. Roosevelt's advice calls to mind a friend of mine who met a fellow on the outdoor patio, aka cigar lounge of a Savannah area restaurant a while back. The man was in Georgia with some buddies who had all brought their street-model race cars to a Savannah area track, which they had rented for a couple days.

When asked the purpose of their get together, he explained that they were all about the same age (mid-60's) and had come there to do hot laps in the company of driving instructors for the express purpose of building skill and "scaring the hell out of themselves." His was a very nice, late model Porsche that happened to be in the parking lot.

The next day he returned to the restaurant and saw the same guy again (sitting in the same chair, and probably smoking the same cigar from the day before.) Upon noticing that the car appeared no worse for wear, he asked the fellow if he had accomplished his objective.

He said that he certainly had, and recounted how, in the company of one of the pro drivers, he had powered into a curve at 130 mph at which point the car got loose and proceeded to do high speed donuts (remaining upright, thankfully) through the infield grass. Upon coming to a stop, he asked the pro driver why he had let him do that and was reminded that it was on his bucket list. Check.

It needn't be loud, ebullient confidence gained at 130 mph, but leadership, the act of getting others to follow and support you in pursuit of some endeavor requires confidence, on your part, and theirs. The people around you must believe that you know what you are doing, that you have their best interests at heart, that there is a reasonable prospect of success, and that no unforeseen harm will come to them by virtue of the association. Absent that, they want nothing to do with you in today's workspace.

Make no mistake, that's a heavy burden because it applies individually with each person on your team. They decide one at a time, and one moment at a time whether you've passed the test and are worthy of their followership.

These assurances come mainly from their reading of your level of confidence, as exhibited by your body language, speech mannerisms, and degree of comfort in your own skin. Further, both your internally felt and externally displayed confidence will be best fed by the pursuit of skill and insight that provide a reasonable basis for being confident. You can't make it up! Very few of us can fake it for long. We're just not good enough actors or actresses. **Being competent provides a primary basis for confidence.**

I'm not suggesting that leaders should attend happy, happy school, but I do maintain that we should work hard at maintaining the knowledge, skill, and insight which lead to heightened levels of confidence and an assured demeanor. Leadership is a craft that, in and of itself requires study... work, and, believe it or not, practice.

As noted above, former First Lady of the United States, Eleanor Roosevelt suggested, "doing one thing every day that scares you." As perversely counterintuitive as that may seem, when we try new things, survive the experience, and occasionally master them, we're stretching and growing our awareness, skill, and yes, confidence.

I think often of my father whom I never really got to know directly (he died when I was 16 months old), but whom I am quite familiar with by virtue of having peppered my Mother with questions about him and having studied his life and accomplishments by reading his papers, letters, talking to those who knew him, and perusing West Point yearbooks from his era. Even without f2f time, these experiences have doubtless helped me become the person I am.

In addition to dad's military role as an aviator, he was a competitive diver and serious candidate for the US Olympic men's diving team. Somewhat analogous to gymnastics, diving requires hundreds of hours of practice to truly be competent and competitive. To do it at a level that would qualify one for Olympic competition certainly requires some x-factor of skill. Whereas falling off a diving board doesn't take much skill or effort, performing complex dives in a highly artistic manner does.

Not unlike diving, piloting an aircraft takes knowledge acquired by training on flight systems/mechanics and considerable practice. Several years ago, as a senior exec with Delta's lead bank, I was treated to a tour and demonstration of one of the flight simulators used by Delta Air Lines for pilot training and certification. Aside from being wowed by what is, without doubt, the ultimate video game, I came away with real appreciation for the x-factor that sims no doubt bring to that arena. Consider for example that today a pilot can get hundreds of hours of practice without needing to tie up an aircraft that's burning fuel and earning no money, or another pilot to be in the seat next to them.

After the demo which was most impressive, I couldn't help but flash back to my dad's crash and wonder whether the outcome would have been the same if he had gotten the same level of training and practice at the end of WW2 that Delta's pilots (and others) get today.

Recalling my own experiences where I've either had, or lacked confidence in a situation, the central common denominator in nearly every case has been my degree of preparation. That's true whether I was taking a test, engaged in a meeting, doing a speech, sales call, using a new set of golf clubs, or just doing something for the first time.

Public speaking is terrifying for many, perhaps most people. Generally, that's not due so much to the fact that you have an audience, an important audience perhaps, as it is to the fact that you're just ill-prepared. You're unsure of what you're going to say, and how you can best say it. Hence, like a criminal with a microphone, we look at our feet instead of our audience, hurriedly mumbling our barely audible words, every third sound being, "umm", shuffling about with hands in our pockets, praying that we won't pass out before we get to the end.

I've heard a lot of crummy presentations and given a few. Preparation matters, a lot, and that includes keeping one's skills in top form. Good public speakers regularly videotape their presentations. They take the video home, watch it, puke, practice some more, and get better.

This book was written amidst the 2021 Olympics in Tokyo. During the games, much attention was called to the women's gymnastics team, and in particular, the story surrounding Simone Biles who is arguably the best competitive gymnast ever, and her decision to withdraw from several competitive events due to what gymnasts refer to as the "twisties." According to Ms. Biles, the twisties are *"the strangest, weirdest feeling"* that makes it almost impossible to tell your up from down.

When you watch a competitive gymnast of her caliber, performing maneuvers that are nearly indescribable with multiple high-speed twists and rotations ending in a smooth upright landing on their feet (sometimes on a narrow wooden beam four feet off the floor,) you can't help but wonder how in the world do they do that? Once again, the answer is simple, they practice, virtually nonstop. I dare say that they experience thousands of hours of practice for every minute of performance in a competition. Sometimes all that work takes a toll, but not unlike gymnasts, leaders must be prepared to put the time in to hone our skills to the point that it becomes evident that others' confidence in us is well-placed, and that we're worth the price of the ride.

Say Less... Say It Better

Too often, we feel under the gun to offer an opinion about something before we even have one, and then wind up saying something sub-optimal or just downright stupid that we can't retract. Don't think for a second that hasn't crossed my mind a few times in the course of writing this book. ☺

More often than not, an extra ounce, or hour, or day or two of preparation would allow us to frame and present a much more cogent point of view, and to do it well. Take the time to read up on something, ask an expert, rehearse that presentation, not until you get it right, but until, like Simone Biles, you *can't* get it wrong! Absent such preparation, sometimes the very best thing to say is nothing, or "I don't know", followed immediately by the words, "but I will find out", as New Zealand Prime Minister, Jacinda Ardern did when first asked about the island nation's longer-term plans for battling Covid-19.

Something that we too often lose sight of is that the folks on our teams don't expect, let alone require perfection. They know we're human and expect us to occasionally screw up. But when we do, they expect us to look them in the eye and own it. That's all. It's not an unfair burden. In fact, being big enough to readily admit our own mistakes provides a template for them by which they can do the same. And that's good - It means we have a much better chance of being a learning, adaptive organization that swings freely (aka Jaywalks) because people aren't terrified of making a mistake.

WHAT?

1. Confidence is a barometer by which others judge the relative safety of interacting with and depending upon us.

2. Preparedness is a major factor by which we raise or reduce our confidence, and the perception thereof.

3. The better leaders I've worked with and for have been those who trust themselves and the people around them to have the resilience and the good sense to learn from mistakes and keep moving.

SO WHAT?

1. Public speaking is both a requirement of those in leadership roles AND a confidence crucible. We don't have to like it, but we do have to master the basics, which can not, repeat, can not be done at the last minute.

2. Don't feel compelled to have every answer. Oftentimes, saying nothing, or "I don't know" can be the best thing to do. It can relieve a lot of pre-game jitters.

NOW WHAT?

1. People don't expect you to be perfect, but they do expect you to be prepared, and to be genuine. When you step in it, say so and clean up your mess. That example helps create a more honest, free swinging, more adaptive organization, capable of Jaywalking. People who are deathly afraid of making a mistake never step off the curb and into the street.

2. Don't allow yourself to become arrogant, or afraid to say, "I don't know, but I will find out and get back to you." Put in place the mechanisms to make sure you reliably do just that.

3. Always put the time in to be prepared. Top professionals in every walk of life (actors, athletes, musicians, speakers, et al) all practice much more than they perform. Look for opportunities throughout your day to stretch, grow, practice, and yes, on occasion, to scare yourself a little. That's what life is for.

Chapter 20:
ORGANIZED
(Who's on First?)

ORGANIZATION

When the University of Alabama Crimson Tide clinched the 2021 College Football Playoff National Championship with a 52-24 win over Ohio State, the win gave coach, Nick Saban seven national titles (six at Alabama), and solidified him as one of the greatest coaches in college football history.

Some may argue about whether or not Saban is college football's best coach, but there is no disputing the fact that he's its best organizer. His assistants and support staff are in his opinion the keys to success. In a nutshell, they are the keepers of the system.

While Coach Saban is the CEO and the players are the frontline, his staff is the organization's core, the glue, and the key to its long-term success. Saban has perhaps the best organization in all of college sports, arguably better even than some pro teams (where he has also coached). He prioritizes their development and is known as a talent farm for other schools and professional leagues alike.

But it goes far beyond the coaching staff to every detail that makes up his system - from the gleaming faucets in the team's immaculately clean locker room to the daily practices which are timed obsessively, down to the second. Year after year, team after team; his system works because the core works. That's why many of his former assistants are now successful head coaches of top programs.

So it goes with any organization. If you want to win, build your middle management - your organization's core. Identify your high-potential people and invest your time, attention, and resources in them. Here's how:

Take Control Of Your Organization's Hiring Process

Start by defining who and what you're looking for. What personality, attitude, skills, education, values, and experience do you need at the foundation of your organization, irrespective of job title? Use these criteria to identify high-potential people both inside and outside your four walls. Put special emphasis on so-called "soft skills."

Promote from within whenever possible. Repeat, *promote from within whenever possible*. Search outside if you must. Make sure HR and middle management understand, *really* understand what you're looking for, and take a direct interest in every hiring decision. Leaders everywhere are prone to running around telling the world that "people are their most important asset." This is a good place to breathe life into that bromide and act like it. Start by spending more than fifteen minutes getting to know someone before you ask them to join your team.

Install A Formal Training System

Have a clear onboarding process and training system for every part of the organization. Don't skimp. Invest your own time in it, arranging for copious amounts of face time with new hires.

Identify high performers early on and rotate them through different functions and parts of the organization. Make sure they understand that being "special" translates to duty, not privilege. Use this system to find and nurture the unsung heroes on your team. Train them in team building, transparency, accountability, and other fundamentals of leadership. Better yet, be a model for those things.

Stay Connected To Your Frontline

As in football, you win or lose on the front line. Coaching and leading are intensely personal. Early on, coach Saban meets with each young player, having him outline his long-term goals for school, football, and beyond. As a coach, he uses this knowledge of their personal goals and vision to help them achieve the focus and discipline - doing what they may not want to do and refraining from doing what they know they shouldn't - to enable success in things they've declared to be important to them.

Make time to buck up those who are having a tough time or otherwise struggling. As General Zais said about his air crews in Vietnam, go sit with them for a few minutes, you don't even have to say anything. They'll know you appreciate them, and it will mean the world to them.

Coach Saban gains insight and credibility by working out with his secondary position players. You are encouraged to do no less with your new teammates. Get to know them well as both professionals and people. What are they good at? What do they do for fun? What's *really* important to them? What scares them?

Get out of your office regularly and meet your 'players' on their turf. Ask questions. Listen. Pay attention. Laugh with them. What do they see and know that you don't? What kind of systemic defects are keeping them from doing their best work, and generally making them crazy? Who in the organization is being especially helpful to your team? Find out, and personally go thank them.

In the bowels of every ship, every organization, you will find a handful of people who regularly and reliably make a huge difference to keep things running smoothly. Know who they are, thank them, invest in them. Praise them to people two or more levels above them in the organization. Never take them for granted!

Stay Connected To Your Network

I'm fond of saying that life is a contact sport - it's one of my favorite analogies. Everyone you meet, every single day represents a potential opportunity, personally or professionally down the road. In fact, every single career opportunity that I've had in my life has come from someone I knew or from some relationship I made where someone was thinking about me or told someone else about me. Few things are more important than the network of friends, colleagues, and others you build in life. Here's how to maximize the value of interpersonal relationships.

Embrace Six Degrees Of Separation

You may have heard the expression "six degrees of separation." If you haven't, it basically refers to the fact that everyone in the world is literally only six clicks away from you in terms of who they know. In business, networking and building relationships is key because there is always a time when you can use advice, an introduction, reference, or simple contact.

Smile, shake hands (or exchange elbow bumps ☺), and build relationships with people. Know their names and something about them. Look for ways that you can "pay it forward" by being of service to them, not as a down payment on a transaction, but a genuine way of trying to create relationships. These are the people who will be your partners as you navigate your interpersonal network of contacts. It's an absolute truism that who you know can be far more worthwhile than *what* you know.

Keep Detailed Information

Keeping detailed contact information for every person you meet is a good habit to adopt and a smart strategy for success. It's easier than ever, our phones and contact managers are crying out to be fed! Not only will you have information available when you need it, but you can stay on top of things when it comes to establishing genuine connections with people.

Does your son play baseball with the child of the woman from the office next to yours? Engage her in conversation about the game. If your sister-in-law knows your neighbor's birthday, write it down and be first to acknowledge it on their special day. It takes next to nothing to send a congratulatory email, text, better yet, old fashioned, handwritten card. Trust me, nobody ever gets mad when you send them one!

Detailed contact information gives you an edge with the people you already know and builds your information toolkit for new people you meet. Make certain to get both the correct spelling and pronunciation of people's names. Know where they work, a little about what they do - their birthday, and preferred mode of contact. The more you know, the higher the likelihood you will foster a truly memorable and genuine connection. As but an example, I try to be aware of when and how people are most receptive to messaging. A word of caution: Don't be creepy by in any way abusing the trust.

Exercise Respect

Athenian philosopher, Plato is credited with saying, "Be kind, for everyone you meet is fighting a hard battle." It's true and that goes for the entry-level mail clerk as well as the person in the corner office, both environments I'm familiar with.

Treat everyone with dignity and respect regardless of their level in the organization or status in life. Give credit and have time for others. You never know when someone will play an important role in your life or when you'll play a key role in theirs. Be caring, compassionate, and inspire trust with everyone. It's good business practice and it's a wonderful human quality.

Building interpersonal relationships and a solid network of friends and business contacts will help you throughout life. Whether you are a janitor or an investment banker, maximize your relationships by being open to meeting new people, really getting to know them, and treating everyone well. Life is indeed a contact sport; it's time to start building that team.

Maintain A Circular Flow Of Information

Be sure your middle managers stay connected both up and down the ladder. As much as possible create a seamless interface between them and you and your frontline. Keep everyone so informed and aware that they will intuitively do their job as you would do it. No, *better* than you would do it.

Build A Culture That Prioritizes Development Of People

Invest in opportunity. You don't just want employees. You want people who can lead, inspire, and motivate others; people who can thrive, not just live in your organization. Provide potential leaders with continuing education and personal development opportunities. Send them to leadership schools. Encourage their participation in relevant professional organizations. Let them know their growth is important by investing in them. *Make serious chunks of your personal time available to them.* Remember that millennials are motivated less by the size of their paycheck than by the significance of the organization's mission, their own work, and the opportunity to grow.

> "Surround yourself with great people. Learn to delegate early on— not trying to do everything yourself. Make sure you've got the kind of people who are praising the team around them, not criticizing. And having people who are willing to really innovate, be bold, and create something that everybody who works for the company can be really proud of."
>
> Sir Richard Branson - told to David Rubinstein

Ultimately, whether you're building a legacy or hoping to sell, the worth of your business will rest largely on the shoulders of the talent in the middle… your core leaders. For your organization's long-term health, build that core. Do it in good times and bad, always keeping your door, your ears, and your heart open.

In Transition

All of us as leaders have assumed new leadership roles on at least one occasion. Congratulations if you're in a new leadership position now. You're embarking on what can be a time of great personal and professional growth — as long as you take it step by step and follow a few basic principles. Having been through the experience several times, I'd like to share with you some of what has worked (and not worked) for me.

One of my biggest challenges occurred when I transitioned from the board of directors to the CEO role at one of the world's largest privately owned real estate publishing and printing companies during a time of enormous technological change. My task was to take an overhead-heavy traditional printer (think big, clunky machines) into the internet age. At the age of 49, it was my third CEO position.

During a 7-year period, we totally right-sized the company, grew revenues by 250%, increased profits sixteen-fold, added 75 net new jobs, and eventually sold the business to a private equity firm. That period confirmed for me several important principles of successful leadership transition.

First and foremost, being thrust into a leadership role makes you neither a leader nor a genius. Let me repeat that… A title doesn't make you, or anyone a leader, and it doesn't compel anyone to respect or follow you. The quicker we all grasp this tenet, the better. That said, when you're hired to effect change that involves convincing lots of hearts and minds to pursue a different path without hesitation, a leader (rather than a manager) is what you need to be.

To me, leadership success is contingent upon the earned consent of those who would follow you. Getting off on the right foot as a leader in transition is essential, and in my experience consists of four phases:

Learn

Start by learning as much as you can. Talk with the previous leader(s), if possible, about what worked and what didn't. Talk with people at the grassroots level — employees, vendors, and customers — even competitors about what they like and don't like. What ideas do they have? Where are the opportunities in the organization, the hidden gems?

Get a sense of the past, (history, culture, key decisions), and what's already there. This process requires you to ask questions, and then have the good sense to shut up and listen, *really* listen to people; not just to what they are saying, but as importantly, what they *aren't* saying, and what they are really emotional about. What are they particularly proud, or scared of? What things do they find especially annoying?

Make certain that you have a complete grasp of the culture, don't disrespect it, and if you need to amend it, do so thoughtfully, respectfully, and in a measured fashion, with your eyes and ears wide open.

Ask them to play king/queen for a day and tell you one thing that they would start and/or stop if they were calling the shots. If they don't have an answer off hand, ask them to go sleep on it and send it to you, because you really want to know. Ask them, for example, what are the things that are driving them crazy, and keeping them from doing their best work. Who's being especially helpful to them? Find out and go thank them. Do it personally.

Assess

Be careful about first impressions. Don't go in spring-loaded to aim and shoot, but if the situation is dire, be a quick study. Assess your talent. Is it matched to the challenge? If not, are there people in the organization who could be part of the leadership team? What changes will you need to make in structure, process, technology, customer experience, leadership, culture, and vendor relations?

Again, be especially thoughtful and deliberate about messing with the culture. That's like doing a heart/lung transplant. It's tricky, It's the very fabric of the institution, and you've got to know what you're doing. You've got to break a few eggs, but you mustn't break the omelet, the fabric of the institution.

Communicate

Most people resist change of any sort, especially when they don't understand what's happening, let alone why. So, as you get your bearings, start communicating, thoughtfully, honestly. People know change is coming, but not the magnitude, direction, or the pace. Be sensitive to their apprehension. Communicate the state and direction of the business clearly and take pains to relate it to each person and work unit in terms and in a manner that suits them.

Use whatever means of communication you have such as in-house blogs or intranets, all-hands meetings, private lunches, company-wide video conferences, whatever it takes. Don't be foolish enough to think that you can say it once and cross it off your list. Your messaging must pierce a lot of competing noise, apprehension, and counter-messaging. Indeed, for at least the first six months, this messaging must be among your primary tasks. You'll probably need to spend two-thirds of your time on it. That's right, two-thirds.

I went old school for part of my presentation and created a simple pocket card that listed the five things (priorities) all of us needed to focus on. If I had it to do over again, I would have asked teammates to commit the items on the card to memory, then ask for the cards back, after which, in an appropriate way, we would quiz people on the focus items, offering prizes for correct answers, and extra reinforcement for leaders where the message hadn't been well reinforced.

Act

Whatever actions you need to take, be fair, decisive, and quick. If job reductions are necessary, don't drag them out. Get it over with, all of it, preferably at one time. In my case we said goodbye to 20% of the workforce in a single day, but when we were done, we were able to tell the remaining team members that we didn't expect any more.

When you must reduce staff, do it with integrity and leave the departing employees with their self-esteem intact while assisting them in their new job search. If able, provide severance, references, and some measure of outplacement assistance. If you have good people with special skills doing obsolete jobs, try to find them other roles in the company. Hold everyone accountable including yourself. Every person who can reasonably be retrofitted into a vacant position should at least be offered the opportunity.

It should be taken for granted that when you're passing out pain, leaders should get more than their share, starting with you. It goes with the territory.

As you're going through that process, bear in mind that everyone is taking note of how you are dealing with their departing teammates and forming the assumption that you would likely deal with them in the same manner. Should you be foolish enough to treat people in an inconsiderate or hostile manner, the remaining staff, the folks you're counting on to make this thing work going forward, will be worrying more about their own future, and getting treated in the same manner. You would be, too. Guess who they won't be worrying about? The word starts with a "C."

Perhaps the most important point to remember is that you can't be a leader without followers. You must earn your new team's trust and respect. So, keep your eyes, ears, mind, and heart (yes, heart) open.

When You're the One Who Has Been Terminated

Let's recognize one fact of life: The higher up the career ladder you go, the greater the chance is that someday you will be "de-selected", likely more than once.

Don't clutter your head for even a nanosecond with the "woe is me" stuff. Everybody who has done anything of significance has had their horse shot out from underneath them at least once: Walt Disney got fired by a Missouri Newspaper for, get this, "a lack of imagination." Walt freakin' Disney!

Fasten your seatbelts: Oprah got demoted by a Nashville television station, Warren Buffett couldn't get accepted at Harvard, Steve Jobs got thrown out of his own company by a president whom he had hired! They all got over it rather well, and you will too, but you've got to keep your wits about you. This is one of those times when you keep company with those one or two really good friends.

Though you can't really alter the odds of it happening, there are things you can do to prepare:

1. Upon entering a new job situation, have a candid discussion with significant others about the relative risk involved. That little chat will do you as much good as it does them.
2. Simultaneous to accepting a new assignment, make appropriate amendments to your resume and LinkedIn page (really, take my word on it, don't wait)
3. Even if you're delighted with your new job, at least once a year, take an interview to confirm that there are good and compelling reasons for your happiness, AND to avoid letting your interview skills get rusty. If nothing else, it is additive to your network.
4. Try very hard to maintain at least a 6 to 12-month cash cushion at all times for emergency living expenses. Sometimes the grim reaper comes without notice, and even without severance.

5. Be ever mindful of current conditions in the job market for those with your skills and experience. Who's growing? Who's "shrinking"? Keep track of the movements of folks in your network and make it a point to notice/acknowledge their achievements. Remember, it's the little stuff.

6. Always treat members of your network with consideration, extending courtesies and kindness to them whenever you can. There is about an 80% chance that someone on that list will play a part in your next job search, and you don't know who it's going to be, so play nice in the sandbox. You should anyhow, even without selfish interest.

7. If you sense that your boss is 'losing that loving feeling', the worst thing you can do is to cower, hide, or ignore it. Pick a good opportunity and ask them about it. "You seem a little distant lately, have I done something to contribute to that? Shut up and let them answer, and no matter what the answer is don't argue with them. Let them be as specific as they are willing to and be sure and thank them for the talk. You should get a better idea if there is an arrow headed your way. One thing that I probably would not do is force their hand by discussing the matter with others in the organization.

8. Take a tip from Bill Gates:

"Look for the job that you would want to hold if you didn't need a job. You're probably only going to live once. You don't want to go sleepwalking through life... Look for the job that turns you on. Find a passion."

(Bill Gates to David Rubinstein)

WHAT?

1. Good leaders with winning teams are exceptionally well-organized, starting with being deadly serious about recruiting and onboarding.
2. Coaching and leading are intensely personal, a contact sport.
3. A Leader is **NOT a BOSS**. Repeat, a leader is NOT a boss.

SO WHAT?

1. Most of the readers of this book would do well to look at themselves as Nick Saban does, as a coach who happens to run a multi-million-dollar business.
2. Leaders who fail to devote significant personal attention to the recruitment and onboarding of new teammates will likely not have championship teams, ever.
3. In contact sports, you're going to get hit on occasion, which can translate to losing your job, for good reason or no reason that makes any sense. It happens. If you really want or need a safe job, stay away from the management track.
4. Leaders pay careful attention to their network, certainly to include the "little stuff."

NOW WHAT?

1. Work on your own coaching skills and take steps to embed as many talented female coaches as possible in your organization. Coaching is heavily dependent on listening, and women often outperform men in that dimension by a wide margin.
2. Take preparatory steps to prepare for career derailments (keep job docs and interview skills current, have a reserve fund, maintain key friendships).
3. Keep your radar on with your boss.
4. Whenever it becomes necessary for you to terminate a team member, do it with decency and consideration, always. There is no reason ever(!) to treat someone with disrespect or animosity as they are leaving your organization.

PART 4:
The Next Level

Chapter 21:
THE CORNER OFFICE
(The head shed)

"Leaders have a significant role in creating the state of mind that is the society. They can serve as symbols of the moral unity of the society. They can express the values that hold the society together. Most important, they can conceive and articulate goals that lift people out of their petty preoccupations, carry them above the conflicts that tear a society apart, and unite them in pursuit of objectives worthy of their best efforts."

– John W. Gardner, "No Easy Victories"

Simple Steps to Becoming a Better Leader

Did curiosity kill the cat? Perhaps, but in business not having curiosity is never a good thing. In fact, asking questions, probing, and getting to the truth are all important aspects of effective leadership. But there's more to the story, because great leaders have a skill set that is defined by a few basics. Here are just a few musings on conducting business in the C-suite that, while exceedingly simple, are often overlooked.

Ask More and Better Questions

Asking questions is an activity that too few in the C-suite prioritize enough. It's almost as if we're totally dialed in to answer mode and we don't do questions. Interestingly, smart leaders understand that they never have all the information they need, that they get a lot of smoke blown up their nose in the course of a day, and as a result, they should continue to refine and build their knowledge base with credible input from different, sometimes less obvious sources.

Asking questions is one of the only ways to truly understand why a process works (or doesn't), why something is done in a certain way, and why something else is no longer needed. When we assume without asking, we tend to make more mistakes. Being thorough, being curious and asking "why" makes sense. Remaining deliberately naive and asking "why not" at times has even more benefit. Questions are good; don't be afraid to ask them, often by using simple expressions. Trust me on this… people really won't think less of you for it.

Hush Y'all

But then, after asking a question, have the good sense to be quiet and listen, *really* listen to the answer. Use the 70:20:10 rule of listening versus talking. And what's the 10 for? Glad you asked. That's for a little silence, when no one is talking. Try it. A discovery technique that has served me well for some time is to simply say, "Tell me more… or what do *you* think?" You'll be amazed at the opportunities that come from what you learn. Allow some "dead time" in your conversations so as to give the other person time to think about and then answer or expound on some of those questions.

Absent that unhurried signal, due to the power variance and their desire not to make a mistake, people will tend toward the safe answer, which may not be their best thinking. Let 'em think for a moment and then speak. In fact, sometimes it helps to invite them to "Take your time."

"As a young CEO, humility was not one of my core leadership traits. For the privilege of having those three letters after my name, I figured I'd better have all the answers or at least act like I did. But pretending to know something when you know you do not is faking it, and faking it has a way of catching up with you. Like many first-time executives, I confused humility with a lack of confidence and, therefore, chalked it up as weakness."

— Sabrina Horn, CEO, and author, "Make It, Don't Fake It"

Spend Your Time Wisely

This is not easy for a former banker, but It has been suggested, correctly I think, that how we choose to spend our time is perhaps even more important than how we spend our money, ergo it behooves us to invest it wisely. As leaders, we have many choices, and many people and causes tugging at the second hand on our clock. After all, no one is going to tell you where you can and can't put your time, but let's face it, some choices are clearly better than others.

Some of the critical success factors I use are:

Perhaps it's the banking background, but I try to **invest, rather than 'spend' time**. In other words, be thoughtful and intentional about your expenditure of time. You needn't be miserly, just intentional.

A friend told me about a CEO he once worked for whose schedule was so tightly wound that he was known for walking into a meeting and announcing, "I have seventeen minutes to spend with you", and you could be certain that in exactly that amount of time, the door was closing behind him. Of course, he's also the same guy who reportedly walked the halls at HQ at 8:20A every morning, and again at 4:40PM just to quietly take note of who was there working, and who wasn't. He would never confront anyone about their punctuality or lack of presence, but you could be sure that someone would. To be sure, check up on people and hold them accountable, but don't be that person.

Reserve Time For Thinking

Put it on the calendar and preserve it. Use it for the intended purpose. Thinking about what?

> *"As a senior executive, what do you really get paid to do? You get paid to make a small number of high-quality decisions. Your job is not to make thousands of decisions every day. If I make three good decisions a day, that's enough. Warren Buffett says he's good if he makes three good decisions a year. I really believe that."*
>
> Jeff Bezos

Use Your Executive Assistant wisely especially in calendar management. They need to be fully "in the room" when it comes to your priorities, deadlines, and scheduling preferences. They should be acutely aware of your work patterns (e.g., when you think best, when you get cranky), and equipped with permission to push back if you're getting derailed by others or through your own devices.

Used wisely, they will be an effective additional set of eyes and ears, likely to hear things that people won't otherwise tell you. I want someone partnered with me in this process who has the license and support to come in, close the door and tell me things that I may not enjoy hearing, but need to know. I also expect that each will treat the other with a certain discretion, and when we've had one of those prayer sessions, we will forget that we've done so when the door opens.

What? You don't have such a person? Permit me to push back hard on this item. This is potentially (and probably) the MVP on your team. Get with it. Not only should senior leaders have an executive assistant on board, they should know how to make the most of their talents, and many of us don't. While we're on the subject, if you're stretched for manpower, or are operating virtually yourself, it's possible to secure the services of a professional virtual executive assistant on a contractual basis rather than hiring an FTE. Some of them, e.g., Atlanta-based Belay Solutions, and Innovative Outsourcing are quite good.

Before taking that step, however, think hard about the areas where you need, and are willing to let this person contribute. In a conversation with my own assistants, who have been at this a while, I inquired as to areas where historically their executives, myself included, have failed to use them as wisely or productively as they might. Here's the top three:

1. He (yeah, I know) still uses me almost exclusively as a pure secretary (think pure clerical duties) rather than a business partner with wingtip high heels who can arrange a meeting with a US senator, freeze a know-it-all executive with but a glance, and yes, type 65 wpm reliably, under duress. If I thought he would listen, I could: Be an extra set of eyes and ears at key meetings, offer constructive input to performance reviews of his direct reports, and be an effective "distant early warning" asset when someone is reaching the boiling point, or some important work is about to drop between the chairs.

2. We've got some exceptional female talent here that needs to be finding its way to the management track, but too often they're not the people who are being put forward for developmental attention. I've probably got a little better visibility into that than he does and am a lot less politically motivated than the people who are making some of those recommendations. If he would ask...

3. Most of the execs I've supported are too much of a "legend in their own minds" when it comes to their public speaking skills. That's a bit like kryptonite around here, so I leave it alone. Truth be known, they need to prepare much longer, harder, and some really should be working with a coach.

   It's so bad that, a while back, one of our execs was giving a big speech for a couple hundred people. He was reading the speech, which was probably a good idea for him, given his lack of proficiency. Someone had written a joke into the speech, a pretty funny joke actually, which he read aloud, and all was fine until he read aloud the laugh prompt, "Ha, Ha, Ha" that had been inserted in his speech text as a cue. Then that speech, and he became the real joke. Few seem to want to do the work sufficient to prepare, and despite offering to help them start prepping sooner, they've all chosen to forge ahead and wing it, in which case, I take two giant steps back and still get embarrassed for, and by association with them."

Ironically, not long ago I watched a tv news report of a North Carolina district attorney announcing his decision not to press charges against some police officers who shot and killed an unarmed drug suspect as they were attempting to take him into custody. Due to the obvious lack of rehearsal and difficulty syncing his prepared remarks with the a/v presentation, he literally stood silently for minutes in front of a global television audience while he and his team got their act together right before our eyes. That was painful to watch, and it happens every day.

> *"As a cross country runner, you learn that for every mile you log at a meet, you're logging 50 miles in training. Preparation is everything."*
>
> Bob Chapek, CEO - Disney

Try to take a significant number of your in-house meetings in **other people's offices and conference rooms**, or out of the office, and yes, many of these do need to be F2F. Doing so lowers the perceived power differential, makes you a bit more visible in the organization (you need that), and here's one last benefit… It's appreciably easier to exit someone else's office than to get them out of yours. Walking 1:1 meetings also provide a different space with the benefit of fresh air.

Time has a habit of getting disproportionately directed to our **favorite topics**, to the exclusion of other priorities that deserve attention. This deserves your periodic attention and is another spot where that assistant can keep you honest. (As an aside, I don't know where, and don't want to think about why anyone ever came to the conclusion that all executive assistants need to be women. They don't. Same for leaders, and everyone in the C-suite.)

The key to success lies in understanding how to apportion time so that no one area is in deficit and no one area is all-encompassing. Balance, not completion is the sign of time well spent and until we learn to manage our priorities and time more effectively, we will never have enough.

You have choices. Personal and professional time will always be in high demand. Learn to use it well and the outcomes will nearly always be better. Keep a log of how you spend your major blocks of time, and periodically compare it to priorities that you set for yourself on how you prefer to spend your time. Positive change occurs only after real behavior modification.

> *"The main thing is to keep the main thing, the main thing."*
>
> Jim Barksdale

Situational Awareness

Renowned executive coach, Marshall Goldsmith advises clients to maintain situational awareness, even in "minor moments". In a blog post, he offers this insight: "What I've noticed about successful people is that they are never completely oblivious to their environment. They do one very important thing differently: They anticipate and prepare for what is next, and they do what they can to create the environment they want when they get there." (*One Thing Successful People Do Differently, 4/22/21*)

I liken this to always trying to think an extra step or two ahead, about things that are not fully within my control, and giving at least some thought to contingencies, and associated steps that I can take.

If, for example, I'll be traveling by car from Asheville, NC to Knoxville, TN, and I know that part of the westbound route via I-40 traverses mountainous terrain, is subject to things like weather variability, regular rock slides, animals wandering into the roadway, fog, and limited forward visibility, all things I cannot control, I take steps to gain advantage via things I do control, like the condition of the vehicle and the time of day I will be traversing that stretch of road. I would prefer that it be in the daylight. When all is said and done, Jaywalking usually requires a higher level of preparedness.

"Feets, don't fail me now."

Mantan Moreland

That same principle plays out at work. If I'm planning to promote Mary to Vice President of IT and backfilling her slot with one of her current direct reports, and recruiting externally for that person's replacement, I ought not get too far down that path before finding out if Mary will accept and be pleased with the assignment... and also, who the other internal candidates may be.

Informed Humility

Too often, by the time they reach the corner office, CEOs are tired of traveling, and prefer instead to delegate the corporate flag waving to others. I've done it, still do it, and yes, my back still hates it.

In an April 2021 podcast (*Seay the Future*), former Tractor Supply Corp. Chairman and CEO, Joe Scarlett recalled how he made it a regular habit to venture out of his office and into the field to visit stores and distribution centers for the purpose of talking and listening directly (F2F) to Tractor Supply associates, customers, and suppliers.

"I would head out, usually on a Monday, taking with me a regional VP of Store Ops and a couple of promising employees on the company airplane. We had a whole fleet of planes... They all say Southwest on the side of them."

I applaud his demonstrated willingness to get directly involved in the development of up-and-coming talent, and you've got to admire the humility and good example of a successful CEO who continues to travel in a single class jet that happens to have 150 other people on it. TSCO shareholders seem to have liked it, too.

Moreover, Mr. Scarlett recognizes that it's vital for the CEO to regularly get out of the puzzle palace to see and be seen at the tip of the spear.

IQ vs. EQ

"Leaders who lead only with their intellect tend to dismiss the opinions of others and dominate decision making. As a result, they overpower less forceful voices that have vital ideas, insights, and answers needed for sound decision making. Leaders with exceptionally high IQs often get too intellectually involved and may be intolerant of others with less raw intellect."

Bill George

Network, Network, Network

If I had just 10 percent of my time available to do but one thing, it would be to network. Connecting with people is by far one of the most important responsibilities and high leverage activities you can engage in, especially at the senior level.

For every person you connect, really connect with, there are five more waiting in the wings.

Products and services are sold through networking, and friends are made. It's big business. Speak to people, and don't be afraid to ask them who you should be hearing from, and whom they might introduce you to.

LinkedIn is a good example of the importance of "linking" with others in your industry (and beyond) to learn more and to expand your relationships. It's but a first step, though, and there is a lot of networking malpractice going on where people think that once someone has accepted a link request, they've opened themselves to immediate sales pitches. Think again.

Be mindful of what (and who) you *don't* know in business. Ask more questions, better questions, spend your time wisely, and use the power of networking to listen, learn, to market yourself and your enterprise. It also helps to practice paying it forward with network connections. People don't like and are understandably suspicious of networking freeloaders.

Networking Nooyi-Style

Shortly after her promotion to PepsiCo CEO, Indra Nooyi visited India to see her Mother. During her stay, visitors congratulated Nooyi's Mother on the CEO's success. It soon dawned on her that parents of great workers rarely get recognition for the person they helped raise, she said on "*The David Rubenstein Show.*"

After the trip, Nooyi wrote more than 400 letters to parents of PepsiCo executives, expressing her gratitude and delight at having the chance to work with their family members. Many of them responded to say that they were honored, she recalled, and some of her executives told her, "My God, this is the best thing that's happened to my parents. And it's the best thing that's happened to me." It's the little stuff, *always* the little stuff!

Once, when Ms. Nooyi was making a job offer to a hard-to-attract candidate, she reportedly called the individual's Mother to persuade her to secure buy-in. I might once have said that that takes cojones, but in this case, it's just sheer marketing and deal making genius! How can a recruiter compete against that?

https://dorothydalton.com/2014/05/19/parents-in-the-workplace/?utm_source=ReviveOldPost&utm_medium=social&utm_campaign=ReviveOldPost

Giving More, Giving Better

Pardon my inherent bias, but you've just gotta love Southern hospitality. It is anything but a myth, and more than a few people have come to appreciate the gracious nature of Southern businesses, communities, and everyday people. Yet, graciousness is about more than charm because it's a practical, smart, and yes, strategic business tool. Not to mention it's just a really good human characteristic. Most of us are considerably more productive when we're relaxed. Here are a few more reasons why being gracious should be an instrumental part of your leadership arsenal.

Giving Is a Multifaceted Activity

The one thing about giving that most of us tend to forget is that it's typically a reciprocal activity. That means it's a natural instinct that when someone gives us something, we want to give something in return. But giving is far from a simple concept. In fact, it's multifaceted and in business, you can give all kinds of things. Executives and professionals willingly give information, advice, and often important introductions to someone. Yet, too often we forget to appropriately recognize the gift, and to reciprocate when someone gives something to us.

Giving As a Strategy is a critical part of running a business and an important part of ensuring that relationships stay connected. Both internally and externally, whether it's between colleagues, superiors/subordinates, or even between contractors, effective giving is not manipulative. It's a sincere gesture of thanks. When people feel appreciated, they perform better. As a strategy, giving and receiving makes sense. It's an easy way to show teammates and customers how much you appreciate their contributions and is a smart way to build trust. Remember that giving is multifaceted and could be as simple as quietly giving time to someone who needs it.

Graciousness Is A Human Trait

Again, it's human nature that when people receive a gift, they want to give something back. When someone bestows kindness, it's only natural to want to reciprocate by returning kindness. Having gratitude and being gracious is underrated, yet perhaps one of the most important parts of being human. When we maximize graciousness, it not only makes *us* feel special, but it also furthers our business goals – and that's good for everyone.

It reminds me of "lagniappe" the Creole – inspired custom of giving a little something extra unexpectedly, say an extra beignet with the purchase of a dozen, or a cup of Gumbo delivered gratuitously by a waiter at Emeril's NOLA restaurant in New Orleans. The act itself leaves you with a long remembered good taste in your mouth, especially that gumbo!

What Can I Do For You?

One of the very best things we can give someone is our time, or ideas, and in some cases, unadorned feedback. Gary Burnison, CEO Korn Ferry offered: "What can I do for you?" or put slightly differently, "How might I be of help to you?" Often, all it takes is this straightforward, sincere question. It is appreciation taken to the next level, on steroids. When others know they're being seen, listened to, understood, and appreciated, that's a powerful and lasting motivator.

"Many people hunger for those things that matter—exposure, exciting projects, and great connections," Naomi Sutherland, who leads the Life Sciences team in our Consulting practice and our Boston office, told me. And leaders need to make sure those opportunities take root among the many, not just the few. "Leaders can't open doors for only those who are most like them or who they naturally feel connected to," she added. "They need to flex themselves to connect with people who are not like them and who do not share those same similarities." After all, inclusion is a behavior.

The Expanding Role of the CEO and their Enterprise

Much has been written and said of late about the expanding role of CEO's and business into realms that they've historically steered clear of… issues pertaining to environmental, social justice, and governance causes, in addition to their more traditional purely profit mindedness.

Though their words are more dressed up, they seem to be saying that we can chew gum and walk at the same time, and happen to believe that strengthening the nexus of business with environmental, social justice, and good governance initiatives are among the best things we can do for our businesses, employees, and shareholders alike.

"So, I think the visible role of the CEO—as not a politician, not a statesman, but as an advocate for who their brand is, what their employees think, what we believe in—has taken a greater resonance and responsibility."

Ed Bastian, Delta Air Lines CEO – 5/12/21 WSJ

In an August 19, 2019, statement for *The Business Roundtable*, Progressive Corporation President and CEO, Tricia Griffith volunteered that, *"CEOs work to generate profits and return value to shareholders, **but the best-run companies do more. They put the customer first and invest in their employees and communities. In the end, it's the most promising way to build long-term value.**"* I couldn't agree more.

A look at the list of about 200 Business Roundtable CEO's who signed on to this pledge establishes that there is some real heft behind the initiative.

In his 5/19/21 CEO Daily piece (one of my regular weekday reads), Fortune CEO, Alan S. Murray noted:

"There is little doubt in my mind that historians will look back at the last few years as a significant turning point in the history of business. Most large companies—the Fortune 500—have significantly increased the attention they pay to social and environmental issues, and are more willing to speak out on controversial social and political issues. Critics see this as political posturing. But in fact, it reflects a fundamental change in the way businesses are run."

He went on to quote a number of execs whom Fortune was hosting a discussion with on this very issue:

"If somebody would have asked me (when I became CEO) whether I was going to be partaking in a conference to discuss this topic today, I would have said: 'What are you talking about? I'm here to run a business.' But it has accelerated during the pandemic, and it isn't just North American, it's global. We see it happening across the world, and it has accelerated dramatically." – Patrick Fisk, CEO, Under Armour

"Major employers are investing in their workers and communities because they know it is the only way to be successful over the long term. These modernized principles reflect the business community's unwavering commitment to continue to push for an economy that serves all Americans." – Jamie Dimon, CEO, JP Morgan Chase

"We do need to address climate change. We do need to reduce carbon emissions. We do need a more inclusive society, and we can't stay polarized. And if business can be a leader and help bridge the divide between two diametrically opposed political parties, then shouldn't we take a shot at that?" – Jim Fitterling, CEO, Dow

"We only exist as businesses because society allows us to exist. It's that simple. The moment society sees us as part of the problem not as part of the solution, in a few years, our businesses are going to be irrelevant. They're going to disappear." – Carlos Brito, CEO, AB InBev

"When we have more diverse perspectives around the table, we found our portfolio companies perform better. We've done the analysis. In our portfolio companies, those with more diverse boards, their earnings grow 12% faster than those companies without diverse boards." – Kewsong Lee, CEO, The Carlyle Group

WHAT?

1. C-suite leaders need to get "out there" where the buck starts and stops.
2. Graciousness is a trait that needs to reside and be well practiced in the C-suite.
3. Asking good questions and listening need to be stronger parts of our repertoire.

SO WHAT?

1. IQ must be balanced with EQ
2. Networking is one of the highest yield activities for those in the C-suite.
3. The best-run (and most successful) companies invest in their employees and communities.
4. It's possible to be both gracious and tough; kind and strong.

NOW WHAT?

1. Ask more and better questions, then listen.
2. Encourage people to "Tell me more."
3. Get out of the office, where the action is.
4. Be gracious, always.
5. Try the gumbo.
6. Hire and learn to work well with an Executive Assistant.

Chapter 22:
Toolbox For Leaders
(Hammer, Nail, Screwdriver)

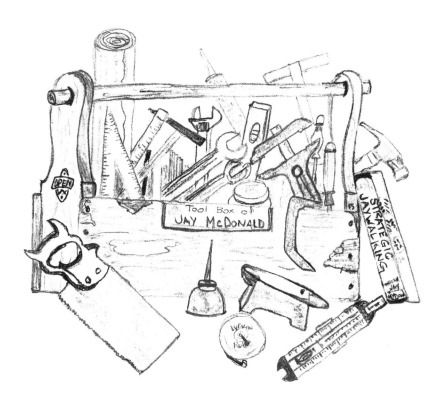

These are rules and tips that I try to live and conduct business by. The fact that the "Do's' outnumber the "Don'ts" by about a 3:1 margin is no accident. People call me a Jaywalker for a reason. I hate being told, 'no.' ☺

DO's

1. Be mindful that you are "on stage" and leaving a legacy (footprints) whether you realize it or not. Make it a good one.
2. Be spring loaded to catch people doing things right and call them out on it.
3. Find a mentor… Be a mentor.

---

4. When choosing competitive weapons, remember your values.

5. Pay attention to the "little stuff." It's always the little stuff. (Indra Nooyi)

6. Tell the truth, period. (Bill George)

7. "Humility is the simplest of all heroic qualities to assume, and yet the least expressed." (Adm. William H. McRaven – USN, retired)

8. Some fires need to be allowed to burn themselves out. A leader's job is to know which ones, and to be aware of fires they've inadvertently set.

9. Bear constantly in mind that the enemy is on the outside, on the other side of the field, in the other locker room. Keep it that way. And yes, every good team needs an 'enemy.'

10. Be the kind of leader that you would follow.

11. Feed opportunities and starve problems. Know the difference.

12. First you feed the troops. Leaders eat last.

13. Make sure that you, your team, and the people around you always know your/their three top priorities, always.

14. Consciously recruit people who listen, smile, care, and say thank you. (Southwest Airlines)

15. "Be Transparent. Transparency makes people feel more like an owner & unlocks human potential." (Bill Gross)

16. "Surround yourself with great people." (Richard Branson)

17. "Break the glass ceiling, the black ceiling, and any other damn ceiling that prevents women and minorities from advancing." (Bill Marriott)

18. "To have long-term success as a coach or in any position of leadership, you have to be obsessed in some way." (Pat Riley)

19. Be ever mindful and appreciative of those who are "packing your parachute." (Capt. J. Charles Plumb – USN, retired)

20. If you're working in the C-suite and, "if somebody treats you badly because you're a woman, it is your fault, not theirs. You have plenty of arrows in your quiver. I have been known to say to people, 'Do you have a problem with me?' You would be surprised how fast people back down if you call them on it, so some of it is taking the reins and refusing to be denied." (Condoleeza Rice)

21. Be self-aware, not self-absorbed.

22. "Always start with the end in mind." (Stephen R. Covey)

DONT'S

1. Don't ever, ever! climb on a teammate's bumper (criticize them) in public. They'll never forgive you for how you made them feel, nor should they.
2. Don't allow anyone to abuse or humiliate your team members, ever.
3. Don't tolerate jerks in your organization, no matter how smart or talented they may be. Help them quickly get to someone else's payroll, preferably a competitor's.
4. "To learn anything other than the stuff you find in books, you need to be able to experiment, to make mistakes, to accept feedback, and to try again. Don't be afraid to do those things." (Charles Handy)
5. Don't wait until you have accumulated all the desired information to make a decision. (Gen. Colin Powell)
6. Never stop selling, or recruiting.
7. Never forget that, at the end of the day, you get paid to think.

Words & Phrases Leaders Should Use More

1. I'm proud of you.
2. Tell me more.
3. How can I best help?
4. What's your advice in this situation?
5. Thank you. I appreciate you.
6. I don't know. What do you think?

Chapter 23:
WHEN YOUR NAME IS ON THE DOOR...OR NOT
(Own It)

When I left banking to become an entrepreneur and business owner, my Mother gave me an autographed copy of the book, **When Your Name Is On the Door** by Earl Brodie. It is a great book about independent business owners, their perspectives, outlooks, and responsibilities. I'd like to honor Mr. Brodie and his book in this space by sharing but a chapter not of his book, but what I've learned after having several decades of experience putting his teachings into practice.

The following perspectives encompass both a business owner's viewpoint as well as that of a non-owner executive. Regardless of which rung of the ladder you stand on, always look at things from an ownership perspective. In my opinion, it's a non-negotiable for great leaders, no matter what they are leading. Take ownership!

Often in my earlier years as an entrepreneur, I'd gather with friends and former colleagues for a drink or just conversation. Often, they would ask, "Isn't it great to own your own business?" My answer, then and now, "It is great, and while literally you are an owner or the only owner of your own business, in reality, the business owns you." Perplexed, they wondered what I meant.

Full-Time 24/7/365

When you own or run a business, you're doing it 24/7 every day of the year. It doesn't vacate your mind when you leave the office or even when you're on vacation. Responsibilities and values don't end when you leave your office. Your responsibilities, stress, fun, and opportunities are always there. No one gives you a bonus or a raise. The business earns it, and you reap the rewards. You eat what you kill.

Although the thought processes are different for owner leaders vs. employee leaders, especially if you've got "skin in the game," your role as leader has great responsibility. The buck not only stops with you, but it often starts with you, too. You're responsible for your employees, their families to a degree, your vendors, your clients, your lenders, your stakeholders, and your fellow owners, if you have them.

When the phone rings at 3:00 AM on a Saturday morning, you answer the call. If it's lightning and raining outside, and you're told the alarm at your building is sounding, you get dressed, drive to meet the police, disarm the alarm, walk the building inside and out to make sure everything is fine…all the while knowing it was probably set off by a power surge.

Leadership isn't for everyone. It's for those who thirst for making a difference and empowering others to accomplish great things! It is for those willing to sacrifice for the greater good of everyone who's counting on them…often into the thousands of mouths which must be fed, considered, and prospering because of the efforts you and your organization are making.

Your name may not be on the door, yet your responsibility and reputation are. Like it or not, you're always on. As a leader you are the face of the organization. Your every action/inaction is observed, scrutinized, and followed…or not. Literally, the leader is "chief cook and bottle washer." By setting the example, you help to create the culture. The culture is what people say about your business or organization at the backyard barbeque when asked, "Where do you work?"

You are strongly advised to set a tone, a climate, that makes the activity folks spend their most time on rewarding, fun, challenging, and purposeful. It's up to you to help your team establish and live in a work environment that will attract and keep the best, most talented people you can find. Success breeds success.

You are the primary delegator of authority but not all responsibility. By doing this, you build your team, embody trust, and serve as a role model for leadership.

The Fishbowl

As your brand's ambassador, you have great influence as a spokesperson, lead salesperson, and community leader. Referrals for customers, employees, opportunities, and investors always seem to go to the best story, culture, and organization. In today's world of social media and instant news, you and your organization are always in a fishbowl. Being mindful of this is always front and center for the modern leader.

New Leader?

When you assume a new leadership role, reach for the largest dose of humility you can find, especially if it's in a new industry. Having done it in different industries as a CEO and board member it's humbling beyond belief, every time. I've done over twenty.

You leave a business that you know well. You know the employees, the customers, the operations, the special language, the industry, the culture, and how to make things happen…quickly.

Suddenly, you're a neophyte all over again. Starting at ground zero, even though you may have a fancy title and lots of responsibility. Become Nancy Drew or Sherlock Holmes. Assume you know little to nothing…and you'll likely be correct. Let others teach you by asking excellent questions, spending time in the trenches, and walking the extra mile.

Barry Cohen, who worked with me at Network Communications, Inc. as the head of our Real Estate Book publications walked into my office on day one of my tenure as CEO, December 31st. He told me they had 32 regional meetings scheduled throughout North America from January 3 - March 31, visiting our 210 or so independent distributors and all company-owned regions. Barry asked if I'd like to attend some. I said, "No, not some… I'll be at all of them." What a wonderful opportunity to learn from the folks who dealt daily with our 100,000 advertisers. It was a gift I wasn't about to squander.

I've always kiddingly said, "The dumbest two people in the world are the one you replace, and the one who replaces you." While that's not true, how many times do you see the finger pointing or hear the blame game when someone leaves and someone else replaces them. Never do this. Ever. When I led bankers, some in new roles would say so-in-so made this bad loan…to which I said, it's yours now, deal with it. Accountability must follow responsibility. Suck it up and do your job. You haven't the time or energy to play the blame game.

Financial Acumen

I've observed and worked with thousands of owners and professionals. One of the most limiting factors for many is not being financially literate. It's critical to understand how cash is generated. Cash is king! What's the difference between Cash Flow and Net Profit? Why are the balance sheets, income statements, and cash flow statements and their relationships so important to understand?

It's because this is the language of business. Your organization's financial story is told through this language, and it's a story you simply must be able to tell and understand. You don't need a bunch of fancy certifications and letters after your name to do this; however, it does take a fundamental understanding of accounting, bookkeeping, and how everything uses or generates cash.

There are all sorts of courses one may take online or elsewhere to gain financial competence. Do it, and you'll be ahead of 90% of the world's leaders. Don't do it, and you'll leave business value and income on the table, all of it perhaps.

It's Lonely at the Top

Leadership, especially when you own your own business, can be a lonely existence. Sure, you've got lots of folks telling you how smart you are, what great decisions you make, and that your organization is perfect. Is this usually true? Sometimes, but often not. All leaders need truth tellers to objectively keep them from being trapped by being too close to the situation, breathing their own fumes, or letting ego drive choices rather than facts and logic. There are also areas and topics where you must keep your own counsel.

Seek out resources which give you the benefit of reality checks, candid feedback, and insights you might not always get within your organization, mirrors that don't always smile back.

Vistage Worldwide is an organization I've been affiliated with for over ten years, currently chairing five leadership peer groups. It is for leaders from emerging rock stars and top performers, C-suite execs, CEO's, and the owner/decision makers in organizations. These peer groups are all from different industries and do not compete with one another, creating an agenda-free, trusting, confidential, and safe place to discuss issues and opportunities facilitated by an experienced executive coach and business leader. The only objectives for each peer is to help one another be the best they can be.

Members receive one-to-one coaching from their Chair and have world class thought leaders as speakers throughout each year. It's an outstanding place to learn what you don't know, while having others who share many of the same challenges to bounce ideas, questions, and solutions off each other. There are other organizations such as industry peer groups, 20 groups, and the Young President's Organization which provide differing leadership learning platforms. Many Vistage members are also in industry organizations.

Boards

One of the questions I often hear from business owners is, "Should I have a board of directors?" The answer is not a simple one. Some smaller firms and start-ups may not have the resources to attract experienced board members. Many may have a handful of unpaid advisors forming a loose knit Advisory Board or just an informal one.

As firms grow in complexity and size, a Fiduciary Board may become the choice. With a Fiduciary Board, the board members are liable to the shareholders/owners to use reasonable business judgment, and empowered to make certain decisions, as determined by the bylaws or operating agreement of the firm, on behalf of the organization. Most operating decisions are delegated from the board to management.

Having served on over 20 boards, I highly recommend considering the creation of a board. It will bring a beneficial level of accountability and thought leadership into your organization. It is especially helpful in family businesses, where there are often personal and family challenges beyond the normal business realm. Having independent, successful, and experienced thought leaders will seldom hurt, unless you don't plan to listen to them.

Family Businesses

Family businesses bring a dynamic into the workplace that can be both exhilarating and frustrating. In addition to all the opportunities in leading a non-family business, the family enterprise can bring complexity via the personalities, rivalries, and divergent objectives of family members. That is a book unto itself.

A couple of recommendations would include having strong buy/sell agreements among the family owners, so a mechanism exists for anyone to realistically exit the family ownership role (applies to partnerships, joint ventures, etc., too).

With respect to children and other family members entering the business from younger generations, I strongly suggest that they spend time working outside the business to gain other perspectives, role models, and real work experience before working full-time in the family business. This will allow them to be better prepared when they enter the business, and equip them with valuable street cred amongst their new peers.

Like it or not, family members working in a business must understand the necessity of them performing at a higher, repeat, higher level, chinning themselves to a higher bar than anyone else in the organization. By default, others will view their role/position as having been anointed rather than earned. Hence, they must earn it every day via effort and results, not birthright.

Hiring, Onboarding, and Development

Many leaders, probably unconsciously, hire folks without having a playbook for onboarding and developing them. It's much like planting flowers and hoping they grow into beautiful blooming plants without tilling the soil, fertilizing it, and providing it with water, sunshine, and other nutrients. Many of your best people leave because of the failure of their leader to provide adequate tools, challenge, high standards, or appreciation.

We're quick to invest huge sums in technology, equipment, software, and marketing, but little in our greatest asset…the real, pulsating human beings who make the place go. While some mid-size or smaller businesses may not have the talent resources to internally develop their folks, there are numerous external programs available to provide such development. You are strongly encouraged to create a serious development plan for each of your potential leaders and key employees. Show them, and the people around them that you care, that you're willing to invest corporate assets and your own time in them. Publicly acknowledge and thank them often. Showing gratitude is never wasted time.

Freeing Up Someone's Future

One of the biggest challenges many leaders have is making tough people decisions. It's never easy or fun. As the leader, your people decisions are a primary way you live and demonstrate your culture. We get what we tolerate. Avoiding making the tough calls is a direct, very public reflection on you. It erodes trust in your leadership.

Like it or not, everyone in your organization knows what is going on and what should be done. The sooner you face up to your responsibilities, the better your firm will be. Problems don't become smaller with age. They grow like Kudzu and can overwhelm and potentially destroy a great company.

When you do have to let someone go, do it with class and dignity. Be fair in their severance, unless they've committed a crime, been unethical, or worse. It's also important to leave folks with their self-esteem. It's emotional for everyone. Be direct, concise, and clear. Neither make nor accept excuses. After working with someone to improve their performance for a reasonable time, make the decision and deal with it cleanly, professionally, and quickly. Folks in your organization might say, "What took you so long?" Perhaps not to your face, but in their minds. Your organization and its people will be better served by your high standards and good example.

Decisions...Human & Otherwise

We hire employees and co-workers, but human beings show up. Many of us in our early careers thought business was all about operations, sales, finance, marketing, technology, and people doing their jobs. It is about those things, but it's mostly about people. People are the lifeblood of any organization. They're your most valuable asset. They are the customer-facing representatives of your brand, the ones who attract your future employees, those who tell your story to the world.

They all have lives beyond the workplace. As a leader, you must get to know their human feelings, thoughts, goals, opportunities, fears, issues, and needs. I'm not implying becoming best friends with them at all. There's a need for psychological distance and mutual respect, but get to know them! An even greater need is for them to know you, and to know that you care. When you can connect with your team in a personal, but respectful way, you create a bond and energy that goes home with them, to your customers, fellow employees, and gets embedded in the organizational fabric.

Sometimes as leaders, we also must act on the spot based on our training, experience, or gut. An example was my friend and Darden classmate, Tom Duke, who as a partner of Sandler O'Neill & Partners, on September 11, 2001, was sitting in his office on the 104th floor of the South Tower of the World Trade Center preparing to leave the building for a meeting when the morning calm was shattered by an enormous explosion and violent shaking as a commercial jet struck the adjacent North Tower.

With a sky filled instantly with smoke, fire, and debris, questions flooded his mind. What should he and his compatriots do? At the time, all the trauma was centered in the adjacent building.

Tom's gut said they should leave. He convinced only four coworkers to leave with him and decided to take the stairs since the elevators had been shut down in 1994 amidst the South Tower parking lot bombing. Exiting down 104 floors was a daunting task. He said, "Go." As they reached the level of the sky elevator on the 76th floor, the public address system announced that all the damage was confined to the other building and that people should return to their offices. What now?

Deciding they'd come this far, they kept going down. A little more than halfway down from the 76th floor, their building shook as if struck by an earthquake, and there was another explosion. While the stairwell occupants had been proceeding in an orderly manner, it became more frenetic, as the pace of descent quickened. About 20 floors from the bottom, a lady was unable to go further. She was quickly picked up and carried down by other evacuees. Firefighters, the true heroes of the day, passed them as they headed upstairs into danger to deal with the catastrophe above.

As they exited through the Plaza, they headed toward Broadway and away from the Towers. Suddenly the horror of the devastation hit him as he realized that no one left on his floor would make it out. For the first time, he questioned himself, *"Why didn't I try to make more people leave?"*

From a safe distance, he watched with horror the collapse of both Towers. It wasn't until later in the day that he reached his family, letting them know he was safe. His firm lost 66 friends, partners, and coworkers of a total workforce of 171 that day. Seventeen of them had made it out of the building. What would you have done that day? In the days following? Over time?

Even in business, leadership is often about more than the business of business. It's about people, their lives, their aspirations, and their dreams. And it's about everyone close to them. Making all sorts of decisions in life and leadership is the mantle of a leader.

Culture

Your leadership along with your team sets your culture and reinforces it daily. Culture is the vibe people feel when they enter your business. I was often told by clients when they visited our companies, *"When I come here, I feel the energy, the passion, and the happiness of those who work here."* Culture is what your employees say about the organization when someone asks them, "What do you do and where do you work?" It's neither rehearsed nor trained. It's lived.

In my early career, I was privileged to work in one of the greatest cultures ever with the C&S Bank. Mills B. Lane fostered a fun, hard-working, always get better, professional, serve the customer well, and trusting culture. Long before voicemail and email, we had phone pads to take names and phone numbers when someone left a message. Each one came with a reminder to smile on the phone, "Get That C&S Smile!" Mr. Lane lived and breathed the culture. It has stayed with me for a lifetime.

Building and nourishing a culture is a lot more than just putting a bunch of posters on the wall. It's about values, people, and relationships. It's about weaving stories into the fabric of the institution and recognizing people who are embodying it in their actions. If it's not getting constantly but respectfully improved, it's getting stale and irrelevant.

Remote Working, aka "Take-Out"

Our workplaces are changing in real time. The corner office is often no longer in the corner of a building. It may be in another corner of the world, or in the lower corner of the "Brady Bunch" squares on Teams or Zoom virtual platforms.

Because remote working is here to stay (the toothpaste is not all going back in the tube), we as leaders must think differently. It's time to get creative and innovative in how we recognize, appreciate, develop, and promote people. How we associate with them. There's an old expression, "Out of sight. Out of mind." We simply must not let that happen to our remote employees. No longer do they get to rub shoulders and often see the firm's leadership in person, having coffee, at the cafeteria, standing next to them in the restroom, or on the elevator…they may only see them occasionally online, or perhaps never!

One of my Vistage members, Peter Green, has an outstanding firm. Most of his employees are virtual and spread across North America. Done before it was fashionable, Peter has found creative and fun ways to keep everyone engaged with birthdays, holidays, and just made-up crazy events to share stories, costumes, gifts, etc. Each of us, in our own way must find appropriate and effective ways to strengthen and nourish the bonds with our teammates.

Innovation

Our competitive environment will be one of facing and dealing with more and more "Jaywalking" competitors. As we see more disruption in industries, technology, and customer behavior, we must develop an attitude of innovation in our organizations. How do we do it?

Innovation comes first from having creative people and creating an environment which enhances and rewards their creativity. Your organization should encourage crazy, out-of-the-box ideas and allow an atmosphere that acknowledges and rewards them. Experimentation and failure need to be a part of the organization of the future. People thrive on recognition and appreciation. So does innovation. Believe in it. Champion it. Reward it.

Strategy, Execution & Storytelling/Branding

One of my greatest privileges as a leadership coach has been facilitating the *Stanford Vistage Executive Leadership Program* for the past five years. It's a collaborative effort between the Stanford Graduate School of Business and Vistage Worldwide. By bringing together the great thought leadership from Stanford with Vistage's leadership peer group practices, we help leaders build their own firm's strategy, organizational design, and storytelling/ branding through an annual program.

Great leaders foster development in these three areas for their products, services, and organization. This is a responsibility often shortchanged by leaders, likely because it's "of the future", and thus deemed of lesser importance than the tasks immediately at hand.

At times, as the visionary keeper of the flame and clairvoyant, leaders must emerge from the weeds of day-to-day and think big picture, blue sky. Strategically, where are you going, what are your competitive advantages, and what changes may happen to improve your uniqueness or put you out of business? Years ago, strategies were satisfactorily handled via five-to-ten-year plans. Now, the time horizons are typically three years or less, and reviewed in some way at least quarterly...it's our rapidly changing world, built for Jaywalking.

Once strategy is set, it must be coupled with the right organization to execute it well. Lots of choices are available from regional, product-driven, market-driven, functional, flat, to hierarchal structures, all of it. Leaders need to evaluate the organization's requirements in terms of people, org design, routines, and culture. Every team is different and must be structured in a way best suiting its strategy and markets.

Finally, leaders are the storytellers of their organizations. Stories are connective tissue. They build brands. As the leader, you should carefully maintain your leadership, company, customer, and employee stories. These breathe life into who you are and what you stand for as an organization. Your purpose and why connects you with your employees' and customers' purposes and whys. They are handed down from one generation of employees to the next.

To be your best as a leader, you must be at once both far-sighted and near-sighted. That's not a suggestion, but an imperative.

Exit Planning

One of Stephen Covey's *Seven Habits of Highly Effective People* suggests that we start with the end in mind. This applies to individuals, of course, but it also applies to leading organizations. It's hard to get where you're going if you don't have a destination in mind.

For all leaders I work with and the boards I'm on, we talk about and work on exit strategies. For a start-up, the exit may be years away. The importance is always intentionally planning all you do for the best possible exit, both in financial terms and in your happiness as well as your stakeholders happiness. Why does this matter?

It matters because we seldom know exactly when the exit may occur, so we should always be as prepared as possible. Sometimes, we receive an offer too good to refuse. Sometimes illness, disability, or even death may cause the firm to change hands. Whatever the reason, if you haven't done the proper things to prepare for the foreseen or unforeseen occurrence, you'll sub-optimize the opportunity. I call it getting ready for the dance, long before the enchanting evening.

In exit planning, some of the things you should be preparing are:

- A strong organization with succession planning
- Good financial records, preferably audited
- A great strategic plan and story
- Excellent understanding of and visibility into your competitive arena
- Strengths, weaknesses, opportunities, & threats, how to mitigate/capitalize
- Tax consequences
- Your number
- Your shareholder/stakeholder desires & interest
- Have well-shared understanding of priorities, and plans for next steps

Doing this from time to time will immensely improve your results when an exit opportunity occurs. It's the best way I know to optimize your future.

After You Sell or Leave

Many leaders after exiting, whether by sale or just leaving, have seller's remorse. They second guess themselves, and it's hard to let go.

My best advice is, you must let it go. You sold it, you retired, you left. Whatever the cause, you are no longer in charge. It's someone else's turn to run it. Be available for advice and consent, **if requested**. Otherwise, exit stage left and get on with the next chapter of your life. Find a purpose for your future and pursue it. Sadly, I've seen many great leaders die shortly after retirement because they had few other interests and their lives had lost purpose. Don't let it happen to you.

Observations:

- Leadership starts with you.
- Understand yourself.
- Leverage your strengths and improve on your weaknesses.
- Define success as being your best.
- Fly with the eagles; never wallow with the ducks.
- Your culture attracts both talent and customers.
- Embrace values, not rules.
- Your team holds itself accountable to each other.
- Trust will be your completive edge.

Jaywalking Hall of Fame

From a long list of potential Jaywalking Hall Of Famers, I've selected two individuals as founding members: **Helen Keller** and **Erik Weihenmayer**, each of whom has worked tirelessly to demonstrate that whereas people may be disadvantaged, they are not disabled. Each of them has crossed not just streets, but time zones, and climbed mountains (literally and figuratively) without the benefit of eyesight. In their honor, I pledge 5% of the net proceeds of this endeavor (book, speeches, etc.) to the Georgia Lighthouse for the Blind and Hearing Impaired or other suitable charities. Reader nominations for future honorees and beneficiaries will be entertained.

Following is a short, incomplete list of some of my all-time favorite Jaywalkers. You, too, have the potential to become an accomplished Jaywalker.

Abraham Lincoln
Albert Einstein
Amelia Earhart
Aristotle
Benjamin Franklin
Bernie Marcus
Billy Payne
Condoleeza Rice
Erik Weihenmayer
Frederick Douglas
Frederick W. Smith
George Washington Carver
Helen Keller
Isaac Newton
Jeff Bezos
Jesus Christ
John Foley
Leonardo DaVinci

Margaret Thatcher
Marie Curie
Martin Luther King Jr.
Mother Teresa
Nelson Mandela
Nikola Tesla
Orville & Wilbur Wright
Rosa Parks
Sara Blakely
Socrates
Steve Jobs
Ted Turner
Thomas Edison
Thomas Jefferson
William Shakespeare
Winston Churchill
Wolfgang Amadeus Mozart

What?

1. We are always a work in progress.
2. Leadership starts with self.
3. "Talent wins games. Teamwork wins championships."
   –Michael Jordan
4. "Teamwork is not a preference, it's a requirement."
   –John Wooden
5. Performance is always a reflection of leadership.

So What?

1. Clarity creates power & connection.
2. Leaders must eliminate confusion.
3. Alignment of values builds trust.

Now What?

1. Create common, clear & concise goals and vision with a strategic playbook.
2. Build conscious independence among your team.
3. Collaborate with the team to set values & standards.
4. Plan opportunities of individual growth & development.
5. Foster a positive, fun culture.
6. Say "Thanks. I appreciate you."
7. Spend time with the high performers.
8. Remove the "cancers" in your culture.
9. Always have an "ownership mentality."

Chapter 24:
EMPOWERING YOUR LEGACY
(Footprints)

In the movie, Dead Poets Society, Robin Williams played an English teacher, Mr. Keating, who brought an unorthodox style to teaching his class about poetry, but in a much larger sense about life.

Keating said, *"We don't read and write poetry because it's cute. We read and write poetry because we are members of the human race. And the human race is filled with passion. And medicine, law, business, engineering, these are noble pursuits and necessary to sustain life. But poetry, beauty, romance, love,* **these are what we stay alive for.***"*

He then quotes from the Walt Whitman poem, O Me! O Life!

"Oh me! Oh life! of the questions of these recurring, Of the endless trains of the faithless, of cities fill'd with the foolish,

The question, O me! so sad, recurring—What good amid these, O me, O life? That you are here—that life exists and identity, Answer:

That the powerful play goes on, and you may contribute a verse. That the powerful play goes on, and you may contribute a verse. What will your verse be?"

We are leaving our legacy daily with everyone we touch. Our actions, attitudes, and even expressions influence others. Each of us is a role model. What prevents us from intentionally building our legacy? From having an influence far beyond our lives?

What Will Your Verse Be?

We all have inherited legacies. The vibrant community where I was raised, the Inglewood neighborhood of Nashville, left me a legacy of making a life for oneself based on integrity, working class values, kindness, continuous improvement. We were taught that nothing was beyond our reach if we sacrificed and made the effort to achieve it.

The school most of us attended, Isaac Litton, encouraged us to do our best in all we do: Academics, forensics, music, theater, sports, all of it. Ours was a legacy received for enhancing our talents, influenced by family, friends, teachers, church, et al We were encoded to be proud, to continuously improve, and to make a difference. Our country provides more opportunities than Any. Place. On. Earth. It's up to us to seize it. As Mr. Keating tells his students, "*Carpe diem, seize the day!*"

The most powerful ten words, two letters each, I was reminded of recently by good friends, John Russell, an inspiration and head of Marketing for Network Communications and Tom Hartman, our outstanding Real Estate Book distributor in Detroit, "*If it is to be, it is up to me.*" Powerful!

Sometimes we hold back due to self-imposed limiting beliefs. Our brains are wired for fear. It's part of self-preservation. Our ancestors avoided being eaten by saber-toothed tigers. Many of our beliefs have been embedded and growing since childhood. We must ask, "Are these beliefs still true?" Here are some of the limiting beliefs we may have.

Not Enough Time

As mentioned previously, we all have 86,400 seconds per day. We choose how we spend most of those seconds. We have all the time there is and should intentionally make the best use of it! How we choose to use it is one of our most important decisions in life. Make enough time.

What Will People Think?

We tend to overestimate the time others spend thinking about us. Get over it. They have their own challenges. We need to live in a way which brings us pride, reinforces our values, and enhances our greater purpose in life. I often tell my grandson, "Don't worry about anything that doesn't worry about you." Focus on what you think and making a difference in your own special, unique way.

It's Too Late

Really? I submit it's never too late until you are pushing up daisies. We have opportunities to positively influence others until we draw our last breath… and far beyond.

Consider some of those who arguably have done or are doing some of their most important work later in life, people like John Glenn, Colonel Harland Sanders, Nelson Mandela, Mother Teresa, Grandma Moses, and our founding fathers. Jaywalkers all! I can assure you that when Diana Nyad stepped into the shark-filled water of the Gulf of Mexico at age 64 to make the swim from Cuba to the Florida Keys, she saw no flashing sign that said, *Cross Now!* Each of these people made significant differences in many lives well beyond their lifetimes.

I'm Not Good Enough

For many of us, lack of self-confidence is a limiting belief which is all too often the product of our own head trash. Take a minute and outline what you do well, both personally and professionally. If you want to extend your research as I did in grad school, ask a couple people who know you well to do the same for you. Take care to pick people who care enough about you to tell the truth. You may be amazed to learn how talented you are. Not good enough in whose opinion? Often, you'll find it is but a self-limiting fallacy, and you can be the master of your own thoughts.

We tend to do what we think. Make your thoughts about yourself positive and realistic. All of us can also always improve. Create a playbook for doing just that. Execute it. I think you'll be surprised by how much your self-esteem grows, and with it, your happiness, and ability to be a positive influence for others.

No One Cares What I Think

What matters is what is true for you, and how you choose to make a difference. It's up to you to make yourself happy! Most of us enjoy being around happy people.

Be Open to Positive Change

By adopting a growth mindset in which we believe change is possible, the possibilities are limitless. Staying in a fixed mindset when we attribute everything to fate and "it's just the way it is, and there's nothing I can do about it" attitude will confine you to a less full life than you're capable of and deserve.

We can stop doubt by reframing our thinking, our habits, and vision. Examine what is truth and what is not by opening yourself to new ideas. Get away from the noisy soundbites of what passes for information and study for yourself. Gather your data, trust your facts, and your gut.

I encourage you to get mentally naked. Temporarily suspend beliefs and engage your childlike wonder, asking 'what if' and 'why not' type questions, and honestly determine what's real and what isn't. Examine beliefs which aren't beneficial to you. You can build a new and refreshed mindset. Create Beautiful You v2.0!

> "The team that has that little boy in 'em that comes out are the teams that do well in the postseason... I really believe that. The team that just plays with emotion and enjoys what they're doing in the postseason, they're really dangerous."
>
> Brian Snitker – Manager, Atlanta Braves
> (2021 MLB Champions)

What If I Fail?

If? *If* you fail? How about *when*? Your path to most significant learnings in your life (riding a bike, tying your shoes, reading, et al) was aided by failure. Notwithstanding some of the glowing things written about me in this book, I'm a failure! I flunked retirement five times. I almost failed out of college my first term. I failed at marriage. Sometimes I fail at parenting. I make mistakes every day. So do you! So does everyone! For example…

The Beatles were turned down by Decca Records because, get this: Guitar playing was "on the way out." Michael Jordan was cut from his high school basketball team. Walt Disney was let go by a newspaper for lack of imagination. See where this is going?

If you haven't failed, you haven't tried much. Escape your comfort zone. Jaywalk a bit. Take a chance on yourself. Bet on you! And always seek to improve.

Perfection is impossible. 80% solutions work. Fail forward! Failure equals learning. Learning equals opportunity. Opportunity equals success.

My Verse

My verse is empowering excellence in others to be the best they can be. My grandson, Mid, is the vessel that helps bring much of my verse to life. I want his life, his peers' lives, and your kids' lives to be better than mine, and any before. There's work to do. With your help, we can make it so!

Your Legacy Journey

How do we continuously enhance our legacy journey? Think of this journey much like a trip in a car. The horizon is always changing as you move forward on your path. The same is true in life. We have obstacles, opportunities, new people, innovative ideas, and a constantly changing landscape. Embrace it. Choose to make a difference!

Find your special calling at the intersection of your passion, your talents, and what is needed in the world. This is your special calling… unique to you and only you. Embrace being positive each day in your behavior and attitude. It's a choice worth making.

Stay engaged in life. Sadly, the least happy and unhealthy people I know are those who have lost purpose. Seek out what you enjoy and pursue it aggressively. Keep your brain and body moving and energized daily. Smile and have fun; it's contagious… be a carrier!

Your Giftbox

All of us have gifts we've received from God or others who've touched our lives. Embrace your gifts. Share them liberally! Don't leave Earth with those gifts sitting in the box, still wrapped. That's like chocolate still in the wrapper.

Live life to its fullest! On his 90th birthday, former president, George H.W Bush went skydiving!! That's living life.

No Regrets

Bronnie Ware, an Australian palliative care nurse, songwriter, and author, studied regrets of men and women on their deathbeds. According to Ms. Ware, here are the top five in descending order:

5. Wish I'd let myself be happier
4. Wish I'd stayed in better touch with my friends
3. Wish I'd had the courage to express my feelings
2. Wish I hadn't worked so hard (ouch)
1. Wish I'd had the courage to be true to myself, not the life others expected of me

> "This above all: To thine own self be true,
> And it must follow, as the night the day,
> Thou canst not be false to any man."
> – Shakespeare, from Hamlet

Your Influence Continues Long After You're Gone

To this day, I'm influenced by my Mother and father, even though I lost him at 16 months and her many years ago. Not a day passes which isn't guided by the legacies they left to me.

My many mentors, role models, and heroes also affect how I think and act daily. Often, I ask myself, "What would Mills Lane do? What would Martin

Luther King, Jr. do? What would Thomas Jefferson and our founding fathers do? What would Mom do? What would dad do?

These are the footprints we will leave on Earth when we are no longer here! Make it the best legacy it can possibly be, and be sure it's authentically you.

You're in Charge of Your Legacy!

In a television commercial a while back, two people were riding up an escalator. Suddenly it lurched to a stop. Looking at one another in desperation, they yelled for help. Though they were in a hurry, they decided there was nothing to do but sit and wait.

Later, a repair person emerged coming up the escalator below them, saying "Don't worry I'll have it fixed in a second." Smiling, they said, "He's gonna fix it!" Then suddenly, the repairman's escalator stopped. Music ensued with the caption: "Most problems are easy to solve. Just get off the escalator!" https://www.youtube.com/watch?v=VrSUe_m19FY

It's up to you, and only you! You control your legacy, your life! Make it intentional. You make a difference! Get off the escalator, Jaywalk a little, and take some action.

In Garth Brook's song, "Pushing Up Daisies," he sings, "There's two dates in time that they'll carve on your stone, and everyone knows what they mean. What's more important is the time that is known in that little dash there in between..." Live your dash! Make it count!

What will your verse be?

What?

1. You are leaving a legacy.
2. You can make a difference.
3. You have special talents and influence.

So What?

1. The world improves as each of us leaves a positive piece of us behind.
2. We have a responsibility to others.
3. Together, we bring a better world.

Now What?

1. Understand and eliminate your limiting beliefs.
2. Erase your fears.
3. Jaywalk, take responsible risks.
4. Have no regrets.
5. Find your verse.
6. Create your intentional legacy.
7. Make a difference!

Chapter 25:
LEADERSHIP THEN & NOW
(A Final Note)

Celebrating our nation's birthday reaffirms the gift of freedom crafted by our founding fathers. This loose knit group of farmers, merchants, and independent thinkers from all thirteen colonies sought liberation from the rule of King George III, manifest in the right to worship as they pleased, and to eliminate taxation without representation.

Convened in Philadelphia on May 19, 1775, shortly after the launch of the American Revolutionary War, the Second Continental Congress comprised 58 men ranging in age from 26 to 70, Benjamin Franklin being the eldest. Fifty-six of them eventually signed the *Declaration of Independence*. Their political and occupational spectrum was broad, divergent on myriad issues. There was a blend of those with agrarian and mercantile interests, varying educational levels, religions, and views on the role of government. Were they otherwise diverse in ways more recognized today? No. Indeed, had women, African Americans, and Native Americans been involved, they might have completed the task better, in half the time, but such were the times.

This band of independent thinkers was united by the quest for freedom from the monarchal tyranny of the British Crown. They sought control of their lives and ultimately the governance of an emerging nation. Their passion and purpose were united for the rights and good of all. Partisanship, what there was of it, was subordinated for the greater good. Bound together in common purpose, many became one, The United States of America.

246 years later, our nation faces an existential crisis, as leadership has given way to tribalism and the "united" in United States of America seems to have gone missing. We no longer command the world stage, have lost two twenty-year wars, despite having the most capable military in history, and give every appearance of a people suffering from ADHD.

So, what leadership lessons might we borrow from our founders and apply today? Eight principles from our past come to mind:

Be Laser-Focused And Action-Oriented On Things That Matter

Our founders put their differences aside for the sole purpose of creating a free and independent country. They didn't waste energy or one another's time with theatrics or petty partisanship. They took decisive action for the common good while rising above partisanship. One person, one vote, one decision keyed to the national interest. Move on. Their priorities were clear and understood. We've got work to do on that.

Have Moral Courage

With the Declaration of Independence in 1776, our forefathers (and Mothers) risked it all, not just their treasure, but their very lives for their beliefs. They played for keeps. Too often today, "risk" is not appearing on a favored cable "news" show, losing Twitter followers, or heaven help us…not getting re-elected! We must match the level of courage demonstrated by our forebears, go all-in, put selfish interest aside, elect and follow leaders with the integrity and fortitude to do what is right, regardless of what might be best for them personally. We mustn't be too timid or selfish to be those leaders, when called.

Listen To Diverse Viewpoints With Open Minds

Unanimity of opinion was far from the case in 1776. Our founders had many conflicting opinions and beliefs. By setting differences aside in pursuit of solutions aimed to do the greatest good, they crafted policies that, while not perfect for any one individual, were workable for a new nation. They did so because they were willing to look at opposing points of view with real curiosity, and their hearts were in the right place. *Leaders listen to and welcome ideas apart from theirs and are willing to give and take to move forward.* On this count, I am heartened by the growing inclusion of women, minorities, and youth in both corporate and political roles of power. The listening dividend alone will improve exponentially.

My grandson proudly affirms that it's going to be up to his generation to make a difference. He's right, but we can help smoothen their path. Our younger generations have talent, energy, empathy, and drive. We owe them role models, education, resource, and principled debate of solutions. It's our duty to grab the mantle, light the path, and then get out of their way.

Get Back To Winning!

Mutual respect and trust are the glue to a winning team, and America needs to start winning again. *Leadership requires treating everyone with dignity, building upon a common bond of shared values and purpose. It also involves holding everyone, but first ourselves accountable as dues paying stakeholders in the American experiment.*

Communicate Openly, Civilly, Meaningfully

Little is accomplished without a free flow of ideas, interests, possibilities. Face to face unfiltered discussions lead to better ideas and outcomes. We have allowed ourselves to be hijacked by the extremes of our political process...the far left and the far right. No one else is to blame. We've done it to ourselves, and we can undo it. If you live in Oklahoma, the "enemy" isn't someone in California, or New York. They're not the ones taking food out of the mouths of your babies.

Speak The Truth

Social media is a communication channel but not always truthful. Leaders must speak the truth even when inconvenient or politically out of step, and openly share it so the public can make its decisions based on facts rather than rhetoric. While we're at it, let's "speak", not shout, and be considerate enough to listen when others are talking.

Care Unselfishly About Others

The nation's founders truly cared about their countrymen. Their "why" was to create a more perfect union. Today, politicians' single-mindedness seems to be toward power and re-election while being subservient to monied supporters and lobbyists. Perhaps we should consider reverting to part-time politicians as they once were, and imposition of term limits; thereby electing folks who are in it for the right reasons, have a naked sense of duty, and a real life to get back to on a regular basis. Leaders are servants who know why they are there, care deeply about and report to those whom they represent. We can do this again.

Perhaps That Is You

Flaws and all, this remains a great country! Though in many respects we seem to have lost our way, I sense that there is still a voice of the people, a gathering heartbeat. I wholeheartedly encourage you to celebrate our independence today, and every day. Send a message calling for principled leadership to your elected representatives, and those who would take their places. Be a leader and voice for positive change, starting right in your own household, your neighborhood. What are you waiting for? The time is now.

God bless America!

Jay McDonald

July 4, 2021

ACKNOWLEDGMENTS

This book would not have been possible without the encouragement and support of friends and business associates who cared enough to commit precious time and energy to the effort. I am particularly indebted to:

Executive Assistants, Cathy DeKoskie (*Chief of Jay*) and Marguerite Parker (*Chief Client Herder*) who worked calendar magic to schedule interviews and book production meetings, transcribed interview recordings, retrieved and edited archival documents for the manuscript, read countless manuscripts, and kept me organized/focused throughout the creative/editorial processes.

- Drs. Ángel and Beth Cabrera for leadership content contribution,
- Bob Hope for crafting the finest book foreword I've ever read,
- Tom Duke, Yum Arnold, countless Vistage Worldwide members and Chairs, fellow board members, and friends who graciously said yes to interviews within their disciplines,
- Christine Vergel de Dios for the Jaywalking Communications Logo Design,
- Fiaz Ahmed for a killer Cover Design,
- Shea Family Artists (ages 4 to 44) who provided custom interior artwork, affording me an opportunity to highlight young talent in a published work,
- Friends who dutifully and repeatedly read every word, and gently (mostly) commented on the evolving drafts of the book,
- Peter Green for having the insight and creativity to suggest the title theme,
- My editors, publishing services gurus and sanity checkers, Bill Catlette, Greg Hastings, and Steve Williford of the Williford Group, as well as the rest of their team…you've kept me focused and on task throughout this process. Your professionalism, wisdom, and experience are unmatched, and I'm grateful. There's a reason you've successfully helped so many distinguished authors organize and publish their books.
- Pamela Dabrowa of Pamela Dabrowa Photography,
- Jeff Jahn and his team at Dynamix for website design, counsel on the book,
- Sarah and Annie Jennings of Annie Jennings PR for guiding the book's publicity efforts, and putting wind in its sails.

Finally, I can never express enough thankfulness to my family, beginning with my parents, grandparents, wife, Jani, our children, Stacy and Sean, grandson, Mid, brother Chris, and his special family. Each of you has shaped my life in so many positive ways. It means a lot.

Special Tribute

Daughters occupy special places in their Dads' hearts. My daughter, Stacy is no exception. Her joy, positivity, and zest for life have been an inspiration throughout my adult life.

Talented beyond imagination, she has Jaywalked since childhood, starting at age six as her Mom and I dined with neighborhood families one evening. While the adults ate in one room, the children played in another. Suddenly, sounds from the movie "*The Sting*" melodically emanated from somewhere in the house. To our amazement, we discovered that Stacy was playing it for her little neighborhood audience on the family's piano, without benefit of sheet music or any musical training whatsoever. She was performing the song because, well… she could! A budding artist had emerged!

Following acquisition of a piano and years of hard work with both dance and musical training, Stacy is now a remarkable professional singer, writer, musician, choreographer, and dancer. I admire her hard work and persistence, and though I have neither clue nor claim as to the genesis of her talent, I hesitate to think when, or even *if* it would have emerged had we rigidly insisted on her 'coloring within the lines' via lessons and practice before cutting loose in song! There's a lesson there somewhere.

More importantly, Stacy's a remarkable person, whom I love dearly, and treasure time together with. She has Jaywalked her entire life, always doing her best to leave her audience and family glad they were lucky enough to catch her infectious energy and enthusiasm.

Parents to a newborn at barely 19 years of age, my wife, Jani and I were thrust abruptly into adulthood. Our son, Sean arrived full of energy, mischief, and competitiveness. Unexpectedly, he brought maturity, responsibility, and joy to our lives as we watched him grow from an infant getting into everything within sight, and now to a responsible adult, father, and business professional. To say that we grew along with him would be an understatement.

Authenticity and character are two of the traits he embodies. You always know where he stands, and that he's consistently aiming to do the right thing. Nothing makes a parent prouder. Nothing.

Sean invests copious amounts of time not only in his son, Mid, but in countless other young people who look to him as a mentor and coach. With caring and sensitivity far greater than God's usual factory equipment, he's perpetually thinking of others, and ways to help them.

Sean has become a man and role model beyond a Dad's wildest dreams. As a father, he's helping Mid to become a great young man following in his footsteps with the drive, energy, and commitment to excellence he has learned since early childhood. No words can express the broad smile Sean gives to me each day!

In Praise Of Grandchildren

God's blessing from Heaven was Mid. Our lives changed the second he arrived...and in such positive and wonderful ways! Having been parents way too early to read the book, get the certificate, and have a clue what we were doing, we got a second chance without the total responsibility. Aren't grandchildren great?

From our first glance at him, Mid has been a dream come true. At once, he's curious, diligent, smart, hard-working, creative, and results driven. He never ceases to amaze! He learned Mandarin in kindergarten, German through an immersion program in elementary school, and he's figured out more about life and the world than most who are five times his age. An outstanding student and great athlete...with handsome good looks (a genes thing ☺) he's got the world by the tail.

Yet, Mid's introspection, curiosity, and sober assessment of the world around him give rise to righteous concerns about some aspects of what my generation is leaving on his doorstep. He often remarks that, "It's going to be up to my generation to straighten this out." I'm heartened by the belief that he's up to the task of leading his peers in making the world better, safer, and happier.

Mid provides me with near-constant smiles, joy, and pride. His precocious thinking, can-do attitude, and commitment to growth will serve him well as he reaches adulthood. I can't wait to watch! Grando.

CURATED QUOTATIONS

JAYWALKING

"Luck is when preparation meets opportunity." – Thomas Jefferson

"My wife and I went to a [kindergarten] parent-teacher conference and were informed that our budding refrigerator artist, Christopher, would be receiving a grade of 'Unsatisfactory' in art. We were shocked. How could any child—let alone our child—receive a poor grade in art at such a young age? His teacher informed us that he had refused to color within the lines, which was a state requirement for demonstrating 'grade-level motor skills.'" – Jordan Ayan, "AHA!"

"Do not follow where the path may lead. Go instead where there is no path and leave a trail." – Ralph Waldo Emerson

"One who is overcautious will accomplish little in life." – Friedrich Von Shiller

Good leaders don't wait for official blessing to try things out. They're prudent, not reckless. But they also realize a fact of life in most organizations: If you ask enough people for permission, you'll inevitably come up against someone who believes their job is to say "no." So, the moral is, don't ask." – Gen. Colin Powell

"All human beings are entrepreneurs. When we were in the caves, we were all self-employed ... finding our food, feeding ourselves. That's where human history began. ... As civilization came, we suppressed it. We became labor because they named us, 'You are labor.' We forgot that we are entrepreneurs."
– Muhammad Yunus

"It is important to recognize that people almost never behave like machines. When given directions, we insist on putting our unique spin on them. When told to follow orders, we resist in obvious or subtle ways. When told to accept someone else's solution or to institute a program created elsewhere, we deny that it has sufficient value." – Margaret Wheatley - "Finding Our Way."

"If you don't know where you are going, you might wind up someplace else."
– Yogi Berra

"Time is the coin of your life... the only coin you have, and only you can determine how it will be spent. Be careful, lest you let other people spend it for you." – Carl Sandberg

"Adaptability is the new efficiency. In the post-pandemic business environment, talent leaders must embrace sustainable adaptability, the capacity to adapt operating practices in a manner that does not deplete or damage resources."
– Kathleen O'Neill

"If you don't like change, you'll like irrelevance even less." *– Gen. Eric Shinseki*

"Henry Aaron became the first Black man for whom white fans in the South cheered." *– President Jimmy Carter*

"When you have a competence that nobody else has, you become more valuable." *– Indra Nooyi*

"Life is a succession of lessons that must be lived to be understood."
– Helen Keller

"Once you have sufficient information to put the likelihood of success in the 40 to 70% range, go with your gut." *– Colin Powell*

"With so much blame looking for targets, we haven't taken time to stop and question our basic beliefs about each other. Are expectations of machinelike obedience and regularity even appropriate when working together?"
– Margaret Wheatley - "Finding Our Way"

"Do one thing every day that scares you." *– Eleanor Roosevelt*

"Feets, don't fail me now." *– Mantan Moreland*

"We set out to change the dynamics of sugar colas in the United States, and we did exactly that -- albeit not in the way we had planned." *– Roberto Goizueta*

WORK & WORKFORCE

"My father had one job in his life, I've had six in mine, my kids will have six at the same time." *– Robin Chase, Founder – ZipCar*

"I work harder at recruiting now than I've ever worked, because you have to do it more often. The top players - you don't know if they're going to be one-and-done, but you know that the really good ones are going to go early. So that means you have to do it over and over." *– Coach Mike Krzyzewski,*

"All the WFH-related toothpaste is not going back in the tube."

"This is becoming a massive war for talent. If you are coming out of this and haven't started thinking about whether your employees are going to be remote or not, your competitors are, and they will pick off your talent." – Jenny Johnson, CEO, Franklin Templeton

"Women want hard jobs. They want demanding jobs. They just need to do it on their own terms and have more control over doing their work. I'm thrilled because there's going to be a demand for flexibility that we've never seen before."
– Dr. Beth Cabrera

"Our people want to read mysteries, not live them!" – Richard Hadden "Contented Cows Still Give Better Milk"

"All of us need to see a clear connection between our work and real, paying customers, or we're likely to conclude that what we do isn't all that important in the scheme of things…"

"Work is contractual. Effort is personal. We give it up when, where, and for whom we choose." – Bill Catlette

LESSONS LEARNED LATELY

"As far as society is concerned…how a company behaves in the world is now as important as what it sells or produces." – Clifton Leaf, Editor-in-Chief, Fortune

"We're living in an environment where we're having meetings in people's bedrooms. Having a high degree of empathy and listening I think has been really, really important through this crisis." – Chip Bergh - CEO, Levi Strauss & Co.

"The responsibility that was shown by all colleagues and workers during the pandemic…they earned, in a way, the right to decide where they want to work and how." – Francesco Starace, CEO, Enel Group

"Soft skills done poorly get hard real fast."

"A leader's responsibility does not stop at the business door." – Kat Cole

"Much has been made of how female heads of state have led their countries during the pandemic — often to astounding success. Women lead a tiny 10% of countries, yet they've come out on top regarding Coronavirus responses. Jacinda Ardern in New Zealand, Tsai Ing-Wen in Taiwan, and Erna Solberg in Norway. They kept COVID cases and COVID-related deaths down." – Angela Priestley

"Never be afraid of the conversations you're having. Be afraid of the conversations you're not having." – Susan Scott, "Fierce Conversations"

"Leaders have a significant role in creating the state of mind that is the society. They can serve as symbols of the moral unity of the society. They can express the values that hold the society together. Most important, they can conceive and articulate goals that lift people out of their petty preoccupations, carry them above the conflicts that tear a society apart, and unite them in pursuit of objectives worthy of their best efforts." – John W. Gardner, "No Easy Victories"

"This pandemic has accelerated time, unmasked those who are in leadership positions, and revealed their authentic character." – Harry Flaris

"So, I think the visible role of the CEO—as not a politician, not a statesman, but as an advocate for who their brand is, what their employees think, what we believe in—has taken a greater resonance and responsibility." – Ed Bastian, CEO, Delta Air Lines

"CEOs work to generate profits and return value to shareholders, but the best-run companies do more. They put the customer first and invest in their employees and communities. In the end, it's the most promising way to build long-term value." – Tricia Griffith, Progressive Corp.

"There is little doubt in my mind that historians will look back at the last few years as a significant turning point in the history of business. Most large companies—the Fortune 500—have significantly increased the attention they pay to social and environmental issues, and are more willing to speak out on controversial social and political issues. Critics see this as political posturing. But in fact, it reflects a fundamental change in the way businesses are run." – Alan S. Murray, CEO, Fortune

"If somebody would have asked me (when I became CEO) whether I was going to be partaking in a conference to discuss this topic today, I would have said: 'What are you talking about? I'm here to run a business.' But it has accelerated during the pandemic, and it isn't just North American, it's global. We see it happening across the world, and it has accelerated dramatically." – Patrick Fisk, CEO, Under Armour

"Major employers are investing in their workers and communities because they know it is the only way to be successful over the long term. These modernized principles reflect the business community's unwavering commitment to continue to push for an economy that serves all Americans." – Jamie Dimon, CEO, JP Morgan Chase

"We do need to address climate change. We do need to reduce carbon emissions. We do need a more inclusive society, and we can't stay polarized. And if business can be a leader and help bridge the divide between two diametrically opposed political parties, then shouldn't we take a shot at that?" – Jim Fitterling, CEO, Dow

"We only exist as businesses because society allows us to exist. It's that simple. The moment society sees us as part of the problem not as part of the solution, in a few years, our businesses are going to be irrelevant. They're going to disappear." – Carlos Brito, CEO, AB InBev

"When we have more diverse perspectives around the table, we found our portfolio companies perform better. We've done the analysis. In our portfolio companies, those with more diverse boards, their earnings grow 12% faster than those companies without diverse boards." – Kewsong Lee, CEO, The Carlyle Group

CURIOSITY

"I went to a bookstore and asked the salesperson, 'Where's the self-help section?' She said if she told me, it would defeat the purpose." – George Carlin

"I think everyone should go to college and get a degree and then spend six months as a bartender and six months as a cab driver. Then they would really be educated." – Al McGuire

"You can observe a lot by just watching." – Yogi Berra

"Curiosity is one of the central traits I look for when hiring, for any position. Curious individuals often come up with the most innovative and even breakthrough ideas that can make a real difference in business. Curious people probe and ask the questions that can make some leaders feel a little uncomfortable. And that's OK, too. My attitude is, bring it on! We need thought-provoking team players who challenge the status quo." – Joe Scarlett, Chairman (ret.) Tractor Supply Corp.

"It sounds silly, but being curious makes you a smarter, more interesting person. When you can ask good questions and show genuine interest in others' lives, people will gravitate toward you." – Joe Scarlett, Chairman (ret.) Tractor Supply Corp.

"Oprah said that her critical skill as an interviewer was listening to what the interviewee was actually saying, and trying to understand the impact of what was being said. I have tried that approach to the best of my own ability. But Oprah has always had a unique way of showing empathy for her interviewees and audience, and it's that ability to connect so viscerally with those watching that has made her so appealing, so unique, and so influential." – David Rubinstein

MAKING MEANING

"Communication - the human connection - is the key to personal and career success." – Paul Meyer

"The other thing is that you're not going to get there alone. Be on a team. Surround yourself with good people and learn how to listen. You're not going to learn with you just talking. And when you do talk, converse. Don't make excuses. Figure out the solution. You don't have to figure it out yourself. That's what we've tried to build our program on for the forty-two years now that I've been a coach." – Mike Krzyzewski (Coach K),

"The one thing I've learned is don't lie to the people... Don't tell your people one thing when the reality is something different." – Indra Nooyi

"When the top dozen people in the organization can't reliably articulate from memory the top 3 priorities, how can the thousands of people who report to them possibly help them accomplish those things?"

"As a person who is sometimes in the room, I think one of the things that I do in the room is to talk about uncomfortable truths." – Darren Walker, CEO, The Ford Foundation

"The two most powerful things in existence: A kind word and a thoughtful gesture." – Ken Langone

"I'm a strong believer that one of the most important things the leader gets to do (or has to do right) is to get the mission and the vision right and to push that day and night, to have a strong sense of why we exist, and what it is we believe in." – Dr. Ángel Cabrera, President, Georgia Institute of Technology

"Never underestimate the power of a single light piercing the darkness." – Roy Holley, "The Power of Moral Leadership"

"In several decades of leading organizations and coaching leaders, I have seen more management careers derailed by the failure to listen than any other single cause."

"There's two dates in time that they'll carve on your stone, and everyone knows what they mean. What's more important is the time that is known in that little dash there in between..." –Garth Brooks, "Pushing Up Daisies"

POSITIVITY

"Nothing can stop the man with the right mental attitude from achieving his goal; nothing on Earth can help the man with the wrong mental attitude." – Thomas Jefferson

"Work like you'll live forever. Play like there's no tomorrow."

"A person without a sense of humor is like a wagon without springs. It's jolted by every pebble on the road." – Henry Ward Beecher

"Great leaders look through the window when things go well..." – Jim Collins

"A leader is someone who creates infectious enthusiasm." – Ted Turner

FOCUS

"People think focus means saying yes to the things you've got to focus on. But that's not what it means at all. It means saying 'no' to the hundred other good ideas that there are. You have to pick carefully. I'm actually as proud of things we haven't done as the things we have done. Innovation is saying no to 1,000 things." – Steve Jobs Founder, Apple

RESPONSIBILITY

"First you feed the troops." – Sgt. Jim Prentice (British Highlanders)

"Make Your Bed" – Adm. William McRaven

"Being responsible sometimes means pissing people off." – Gen. Colin Powell, US Army (dec.)

"Do the right thing, even when it's difficult." – Bernice Bunny McDonald Ritter, Jay's Mother

"Your legacy is every life that you've touched. We like to think that these great, philanthropic moments are the ones that leave the impact, or will make the huge difference in the world, but it's really what you do every day. It's how you use your life to be a light to someone else's." – Oprah

"All of us have the spark of leadership in us, whether it is in business, government, or as a nonprofit volunteer. The challenge is to understand ourselves well enough to discover where we can use our leadership gifts to serve others. We're here for something. Life is about giving and living fully." – Ann Fudge, CEO - Young & Rubicam

"I met my father once. I was about four years old. And-- my cousin brought me by and said, "Joe, this is your son, Darren. And don't you wanna say hello to him?" And he wouldn't come out of the house. I actually never saw his face because the screen door covered most of his face. – Darren Walker, CEO - The Ford Foundation

LEADERSHIP

"What really makes a difference in the world is great leaders." – Bill George in *"Conversation With Dr. Ángel Cabrera"*

"The business of leaders is people."

"People perform better when they know you care." – Dr. Beth Cabrera

"Humility is the simplest of all heroic qualities to assume, and yet the least expressed." – Adm. William McRaven (USN, Retired)

"Humility. It's really important to know what you don't know and listen to people who do know what you don't know." – George W. Bush to David Rubinstein, on what it takes to be President

"As leaders who are influencers and role models, we are responsible for separating the pepper from the fly poo…"

"Don't ever single someone out and climb on their bumper in public…"

"Integrity is the soul of leadership! Trust is the engine of leadership!" – Amine A. Ayad

"Leadership is about having the courage to be right there with another person during their experience. It's not about platitudes or scripted speeches, rather the willingness to be there." – Jennifer Tsang

"I think one of the sad things that I've seen in political leadership is – because we've placed over time so much emphasis on notions of assertiveness and strength – that we probably have assumed that it means you can't have those other qualities of kindness and empathy. And yet, when you think about all the big challenges that we face in the world, that's probably the quality we need the most." – (Speaking of Jacinda Ardern) Susan Devaney

"The most important thing about leadership is your character and the values that guide your life. If you are guided by an internal compass that represents your character and values, you're going to be fine. Let your values guide your actions and don't ever lose your internal compass. Everything isn't black or white. There are a lot of gray areas in business." – Brenda Barnes – former CEO, Sara Lee

"People do what people see." – Joe Scarlett, Chmn. & CEO (retired), Tractor Supply Corp.

"Too often, people are assumed to be empty chess pieces to be moved around by grand viziers, which may explain why so many top managers immerse their calendar time in deal making, restructuring and the latest management fad. How many immerse themselves in the goal of creating an environment where the best, the brightest, the most creative are attracted, retained and, most importantly... unleashed?" – Gen. Colin Powell (US Army & US Sec'y of State)

"Leadership is the wise use of power. Power is the capacity to translate intention into reality and sustain it." – Warren Bennis

"Surround yourself with great people. Learn to delegate early on—not trying to do everything yourself. Make sure you've got the kind of people who are praising the team around them, not criticizing. And having people who are willing to really innovate, be bold, and create something that everybody who works for the company can be really proud of." – Sir Richard Branson - told to David Rubinstein

"As a young CEO, humility was not one of my core leadership traits. For the privilege of having those three letters after my name, I figured I'd better have all the answers or at least act like I did. But pretending to know something when you know you do not is faking it, and faking it has a way of catching up with you. Like many first-time executives, I confused humility with a lack of confidence and, therefore, chalked it up as weakness." – Sabrina Horn, CEO, & author, "Make It, Don't Fake It"

"As a senior executive, what do you really get paid to do? You get paid to make a small number of high-quality decisions. Your job is not to make thousands of decisions every day. If I make three good decisions a day, that's enough. Warren Buffett says he's good if he makes three good decisions a year. I really believe that." – Jeff Bezos

"Leaders who lead only with their intellect tend to dismiss the opinions of others and dominate decision making. As a result, they overpower less forceful voices that have vital ideas, insights, and answers needed for sound decision making. Leaders with exceptionally high IQs often get too intellectually involved and may be intolerant of others with less raw intellect." – Bill George

PERSPECTIVE

"The only thing to fear is fear itself." – Franklin D. Roosevelt

"Being a woman is hard work." – Maya Angelou

"What I see are NOT the numbers. I see their FACES." – Coach Pat Summitt

"There's no team without trust." – Paul Santagata, Head of Industry, Google

"We the people will always accomplish so much more than I the person." – Chef Jose Andres

"Character may be manifested in the great moments, but it is made in the small ones." – Winston Churchill

"If UPS hadn't come along, we would have had to invent them. We're so much better for having the competition." – Fred Smith (FedEx Founder, Chmn., & CEO)

"You Can't Always Get What You Want" – The Rolling Stones

"Your legacy is every life that you've touched. We like to think that these great, philanthropic moments are the ones that leave the impact, or will make the huge difference in the world, but it's really what you do every day. It's how you use your life to be a light to somebody else's." – Oprah

AND ANOTHER THING

"(Hank) Aaron was impressive in terms of having the most resilient, methodically productive career the world has ever seen, while also exuding a quiet confidence, resilience, and dignity, even when dealing with the sad reality of death threats as he approached Ruth's home run record." – Trinity Bland, Ryan Hardison

"We are often led to believe that sentiments like compassion and kindness are expressions of weakness rather than signs of strength. And we are often all too ready to give in to the false belief that meanness somehow equates to toughness and that empathy is empty of power..." – Sen. Cory Booker

"Making no decision is in itself a decision, and usually the wrong one." – Frederick W. Smith, Founder & Chmn. FedEx

"When you can make a decision with analysis, you should do so. But it turns out in life that your most important decisions are always made with instinct, intuition, taste, heart." – Jeff Bezos

"Resilience is very different than being numb. Resilience means you experience, you feel, you fail, you hurt. You fall, but you keep going." – Yasmin Mogahed

"Sometimes you must be willing to risk looking foolish to become knowledgeable." – Roberto Goizueta -

"No one can make you feel inferior without your consent." – Eleanor Roosevelt

"Make each day a masterpiece." – John Wooden

"Never get so busy making a living that you forget to make a life." – Dolly Parton

"If you want to test a man's character, give him power." – Abraham Lincoln

"Be kind, for everyone you meet is fighting a hard battle." – Plato

"Look for the job that you would want to hold if you didn't need a job. You're probably only going to live once. You don't want to go sleepwalking through life… Look for the job that turns you on. Find a passion." – Bill Gates to David Rubinstein

"As a cross country runner, you learn that for every mile you log at a meet, you're logging 50 miles in training. Preparation is everything." – Bob Chapek, CEO, Disney

"The main thing is to keep the main thing, the main thing." – Jim Barksdale

"The team that has that little boy in 'em that comes out are the teams that do well in the postseason... I really believe that. The team that just plays with emotion and enjoys what they're doing in the postseason, they're really dangerous." – Brian Snitker – Manager, Atlanta Braves (2021 MLB Champions)

INDEX

ABOUT THE AUTHOR

JAY McDONALD

Where's Jay?	**The Important Stuff**
Jay@Jaymcdonald.com	Father 2x, Grandfather
Linkedin.com/in/jaymmcdonald	Reading, writing, golf
Twitter: @JayMMcDonald	ATL-area Resident

Business Profile:

Executive Coach, Strategist, Speaker, and Author with 5 decades of leadership experience as an Atlanta-area business advisor, serial entrepreneur, CEO, board member, and owner across multiple venues and time frames.

Known For:

Vision, high energy, quick wit, passionate mentoring. Results-oriented motivator who exudes enthusiasm. Executives love him because he shares their passion, respects their time/confidence, and tells them the truth when others won't.

Leading thousands of teammates to success as an entrepreneur, CEO, and business owner in multiple industries. Active board service for both private and non-profit organizations.

Awards & Recognitions:

Joseph Mayo Pettit Distinguished Service Award (2022): The highest award conferred by the Georgia Institute of Technology Alumni Association, honoring alumni who have provided outstanding support of the Institute and Alumni Association throughout a lifetime, and who have provided leadership in their chosen professions and local communities.

Prior Affiliations:

Past Chairman, Georgia Tech Alumni Association, 1998-99; Past President, Cherokee Town & Country Club, 1997-98; Licensed real estate professional, 1995-Present; Licensed neutral with the Supreme Court of Georgia, 2011-Present; Distinguished Clown Corps, Children's Healthcare of Atlanta, 1999-2002; Atlanta Braves Advisory board, 2005; Olympic Torchbearer, 2002; Governor's Advisory Council for Science & Technology Development, 1992-1995; Leadership Georgia, 1981; Atlanta Chamber of Commerce Board, 1974, President's Committee Chair, 1973.

Current Affiliations:

Vistage Worldwide Master Chair for 5 Atlanta groups. Chairman & CEO of Middleton McDonald Group and Jaywalking Communications, LLC; Chairman of the Board of Directors of ECI Group, Atlanta, GA; Chairman of the Board of Directors of Stafford Development Company, Tifton, GA; and Board member of the Frabel Art Foundation, Atlanta, GA. Keynote speaker and a nationally recognized trainer. Licensed realtor, and Neutral with the Supreme court of Georgia.

Designated Charity:

Georgia Lighthouse for the Blind and Hearing Impaired and other appropriate charities.

Additional Praise:

Without a doubt the best book on leadership I've ever read… *Strategic Jaywalking* is packed with easy-to-read inspiring personal stories, stimulating quotes, valuable experiences, and rock-solid guidance for today's world. It is a fabulous recipe book for leadership success. Grab a highlighter and a note pad. You are going to fill it with awesome ideas for your own leadership future."
    – Frank Feather, Business Futurist/Strategist & Author, "Think Future."

"Jay's mission to empower leaders to be the best they can be comes through clearly in his engaging book, *Strategic Jaywalking*. Using humor and wisdom gained through his impressive leadership journey and the experiences of other leaders, Jay shares valuable lessons that are sure to help you become the leader you aspire to be."
    – Dr. Beth Cabrera, author of Beyond Happy: Women, Work,
      and Well-Being

"*Strategic Jaywalking* is packed full of real-world business lessons from a leader who has not only walked the walk, but done so with courage, high integrity, laughter, and an authentic love of people. No matter your age or stage in your career, Jay McDonald makes an impact on those who aspire to continue to learn, grow, and leave a legacy of significance."
    – Harry Flaris, Founder, Inspiration with Flair

"Jay McDonald has run more businesses than most people have worked for across the entirety of their careers. Through his willingness to put the lessons from those experiences out there, readers of *Strategic Jaywalking* gain valuable insight about the essential elements of leadership and life."
    – Josh Citron, CEO & Co-founder of Chic Soul

"*Strategic Jaywalking* is a refreshingly honest self-reflection packed with lessons learned and supported by an impressive collection of quotes and data. While you'll learn a great deal about the past, his unique lens on business and life informs us about what's next. That's why everyone should read it. Jay McDonald defines jaywalking in myriad ways. For me, it now means having had the incredible opportunity to walk in Jay's shoes. Enjoy!"
    – Leo Bottary, Founder/Managing Partner, Peernovation, LLC

"With practical leadership lessons on critical topics such as cultivating curiosity, the importance of lifelong learning and effective time management, Jay McDonald's *Strategic Jaywalking* distills a host of insights into a highly readable volume."

> – Dr. Scott C. Beardsley, Dean of the University of Virginia
>   Darden School of Business

"With leadership development having become a DIY process and if you are currently in or aspire to a leadership role, you need to read Jay's book, *Strategic Jaywalking*. The takeaways are numerous, highly usable, and well worth your time."

> – Beth Armknecht Miller, Talent Management & Leadership Coach,
>   Founder, Executive Velocity; author of "Replaceable: An Obsession
>   With Succession"

Short on theory and long on practical experience, *Strategic Jaywalking* is chock full of good life and leadership advice. The incisive chapter summaries alone are worth the price of admission."

> – John "Pepper" Bullock, Dean, The Academy WITHIN

"There is no efficiency nor advantage in business greater than working with good people that you enjoy working with. The individual threads of *Strategic Jaywalking* serve to internalize for the reader Jay's experience and convey this important lesson."

> – Brett Goodson, Co-Founder & CEO, Almond Cow

"Jay shares much inspiration, relevant stories, and wisdom in this special book, *Strategic Jaywalking*. His words are conversational as you move anxiously from page to page. Soulful and sincere writing inspires and coupled with a lifetime of proven wisdom in leadership, changes folks permanently. Just as Jay has altered many lives like mine through his direct engagement, he will also positively alter yours through this book. Bottom line, *Strategic Jaywalking* will change you at a foundational level, right in your core where change usually sticks! You'll become a better leader and person by reading it and incorporating its lessons."

> – Bill Blackstock, President & CEO, Resilient Floor Covering Institute

CPSIA information can be obtained
at www.ICGtesting.com
Printed in the USA
LVHW080758050522
717841LV00007B/365